ATLAS
OF
DREAM
LANDS

Originally published as *L'Atlas des contrées rêvées*, ©2017 Flammarion, Paris
Translated from the French by Rebecca DeWald.

Library of Congress Control Number: 2022944206

Type set in Pluto Sans/DTLParadoxT

ISBN: 978-0-7643-6594-2
Printed in Portugal

Published by Schiffer Publishing, Ltd.
4880 Lower Valley Road
Atglen, PA 19310
Phone: (610) 593-1777; Fax: (610) 593-2002
Email: Info@schifferbooks.com
Web: www.schifferbooks.com

For our complete selection of fine books on this and related subjects, please visit our website at www.schifferbooks.com. You may also write for a free catalog.

Schiffer Publishing's titles are available at special discounts for bulk purchases for sales promotions or premiums. Special editions, including personalized covers, corporate imprints, and excerpts, can be created in large quantities for special needs. For more information, contact the publisher.

We are always looking for people to write books on new and related subjects. If you have an idea for a book, please contact us at proposals@schifferbooks.com.

ATLAS
OF
DREAM
LANDS

Dominique Lanni

ILLUSTRATIONS BY
Karin Doering-Froger

SCHIFFER
PUBLISHING

4880 Lower Valley Road · Atglen, PA 19310

For Stéfanie

For Justine, Quentin, Pablo, and Diego

And for Cédric.

CONTENTS

> Happy he who, like Ulysses, has made a fine journey
> or has won the Golden Fleece and then returns, expe-
> rienced and knowledgeable, to spend the rest of his
> life among his family!
>
> —Joachim du Bellay, *The Regrets*

THE MYTHICAL ELSEWHERE

The history of cartography rather remarkably maps onto the evolution of geographical knowledge. The physical design of maps, with their opportune tears and legends, lets us read in them the shortcomings, doubts, questions, and certainties of humankind. Delineating the regions, indicating the location of seas, rivers, and sometimes the inhabitants of a place, maps become more precise thanks to travelers' and explorers' accounts, memoirs, and reports. "Long ways, long lies," as the saying goes. Some countries, lands, islands, entire continents, and kingdoms have appeared in various parts of the world and, in more or less remote time periods, risen from the very regions or, inspired by these, emerged from oceans, or have entirely been made up. These lands are imbued with a mysterious aura, shrouded in legend, and are dreamscapes through and through.

Is the world finite? Where are its edges? These were the questions driving the ancient Greeks for whom the ecumene—the known world—ended with the Barbary Coast, Libya, and Ethiopia in the south; Colchis, the Euxine Sea, the Garden of the Hesperides in the east; and ultima Thule in the north.

In the West, places such as the islands of Kythira, Ogygia, and Candia or the city of Troy soon reached and retained their status as dreamlands. The location of a war that may have never occurred, Troy fascinated the poets of antiquity before exerting its powerful pull on the imagination of mythologists, playwrights, and archeologists. Kythira, the island blessed by the gods, has long been regarded as the island of love; Candia has become known as the isle of heroes and the scene of the clash between Theseus and the Minotaur. Searching for and locating Ogygia, the island of the enchantress Circe, has led many Hellenists to go on long journeys crisscrossing the Mediterranean with a copy of the *Odyssey* in hand.

Colchis, the location of the Golden Fleece, and the obscure land of the Cimmerians, inhabitants of underground tunnel systems, all have been located in the East. Inspired by Marco Polo's account in the *Book of the Marvels of the World* (known as *The Travels of Marco Polo*), which includes many wonders, infinite riches, and golden palaces, more than one traveler dreamed about Cathay, Cipangu, and the Indies. One dreamer in particular with formidable intuition would be at the root of one of the most incredible and fruitful mistakes in the history of navigation and the Age of Discovery. Without Marco Polo, Christopher Columbus would never have dreamed of India, and he would never have found a route to these Indies that, as Columbus's dream began to fade, would be called the "West Indies." Until the seventeenth century, Taprobana was known as the place where Adam and Eve lived and surrendered to temptation, with the imprint of Adam's foot visible on one of the island's hills, which still serves as irrefutable proof for skeptical pilgrims . . . "Semper aliquid novi est in Africa" ("From Africa always something new"), as the saying goes. If the Barbary Coast is a fantasy space sprung from ancient and medieval imagination, it is because it lets us see an Africa that no one would have expected before the eighteenth century: a rich, prosperous, and happy continent. On the other hand, the continent had remained unknown for a long time until a passable route around Cape Bojador, the "Cape of Fear," was found under the orders of Henry the Navigator. After that, Africa revealed a Christian land—Prester John's kingdom; a flamboyant empire—Meroë, huge territories populated by savages, monsters, and freaks; the Congo; Mwenemutapa, the land of the Mangbetu; and a kingdom speckled with gold mines—the kingdom of Saba'. The lands of the Black Continent are not the only ones to have fascinated travelers, cosmographers, and utopians. For centuries, the sources of the Nile have been localized at various random spots, since one of its tributaries, the river Gihon, was long believed to be the river leading to paradise . . .

Perhaps more fruitful in producing legendary lands than Africa has been the New World, from the land of the Amazons to El Dorado and the Seven Cities of Gold. When you succumb to it, the gold rush makes you commit crazy acts and crimes in its name . . . Pizarro, Orellana, Olid: these are the names of only a few of the conquistadors who put this fourth world to fire and sword—a world from which the West still had so much to learn in terms of astronomy, mathematics, and botany—only to capture its cities of gold that only ever existed in the minds of those who invented them.

Because of their relative or extreme remoteness, the edges of the world have also been invested with a mythopoetic function: in the Far West, Mount Atlas was considered the location of the Garden of the Hesperides; at the edge of the inhabited world were the Isles of the Blessed; in the north, Thule, and at the borders of the South Sea was Terra Australis, whose landmass supposedly counterbalanced the weight of the continents situated north of the equator; and New Cythera, this enchanting island in which Louis-Antoine de Bougainville and his crew thought to have recognized paradise on Earth . . .

This atlas invites the reader to explore these and other places, in the company of historians such as Herodotus, Strabo, and Diodorus of Sicily; of travelers such as Marco Polo and Christopher Columbus; and of conquerors such as Pizarro and Orellana, but also of novelists, polygraphs, and scholars such as Heinrich Schliemann, Victor Bérard, and Jules Hermann. It is a traveler's invitation on a journey to dreamlike places that are sometimes imagined and imaginary, but all of which are, to use the words of poet-traveler Henri Michaux in his poetry collection *Ailleurs* (combining Ici, Poddema, Voyage en Grande Garabagne, and Au Pays de la Magie), so "perfectly real."

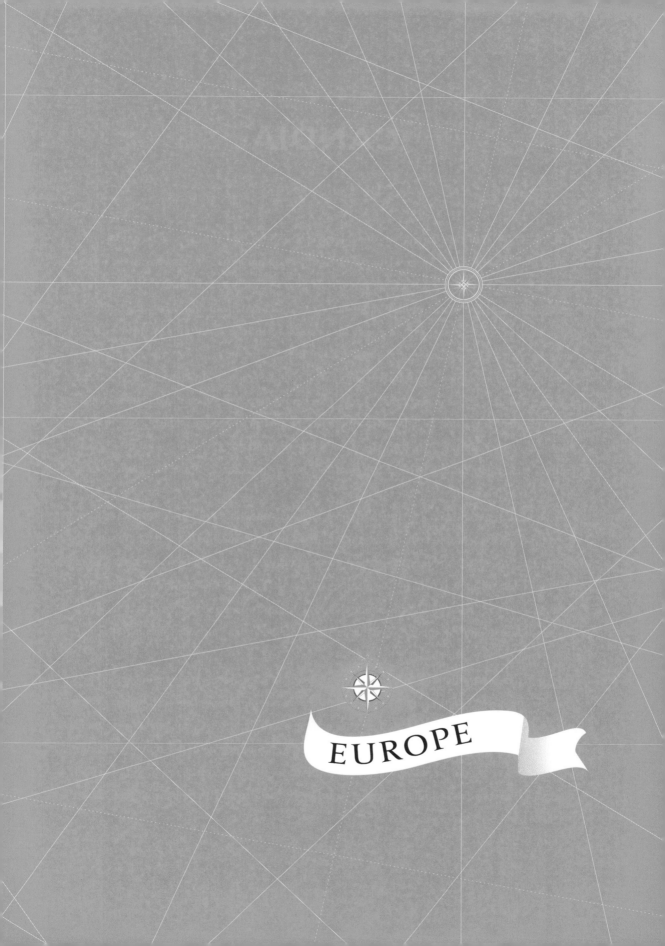

EUROPE

CANDIA

The Happy Island

FOR A FEW CENTURIES, Candia was the name given to Crete. It might have led us to forget the history of this island, which inextricably enmeshes the traditions of its inhabitants with the myths associated with the isle. Who could ever forget the frescoes of Knossos? Dolphins in a still-vibrant shade of blue and kouroi with graceful silhouettes have enchanted the minds, as have the bullfighting scenes that depict young people doing acrobatics on aurochs with gigantic horns. Greek mythology does not leave these practices to the mercy of centuries of wear and tear—not when it's the white bull given to Minos, king of Crete, by Poseidon, which would be captured by Hercules. But for those who are passionate about ancient history, Crete is the land of heroes, the "happy island" about which the cosmographer François de Belleforest wrote that "the ancient Greeks are of the opinion that the heroes all originated from this island." It was on this fertile land that Daedalus, ordered by Minos, built his famous labyrinth to hide the half-man, half-bull monster that Pasiphaë had given birth to after her illicit union with the white bull.

One hundred times invaded, one hundred times liberated, one hundred times reconquered: over the centuries, Candia would be handed from the Achaeans to the Muslims to the Byzantines to the Turks to the Venetians. And it is one of the miracles of history that this land that has been abused so many times still appears to us in the splendor it had when Theseus slew the Minotaur, when Hercules wrestled the Cretan bull to the ground that, struck with Poseidon's rage, terrorized the lands. Besides, this is an oddly prophetic myth that seems to foreshadow the successive occupations Crete had to endure due to its isolation.

This is often the case with those who want to remain free: while the Cretans are sometimes associated with the continent's conflicts in the history of ancient Greece, they always kept their distance from the Athenians and the Spartans. Although they had remarkable athletes, Cretans were rarely found competing in the Olympic Games of antiquity. An island with countless natural resources, and as the expression of an age-old art of living, Crete represents the center of the world, in a way. And as if all beauty were destined to be spoiled, over the centuries the island would become the object of desire of all its neighboring countries.

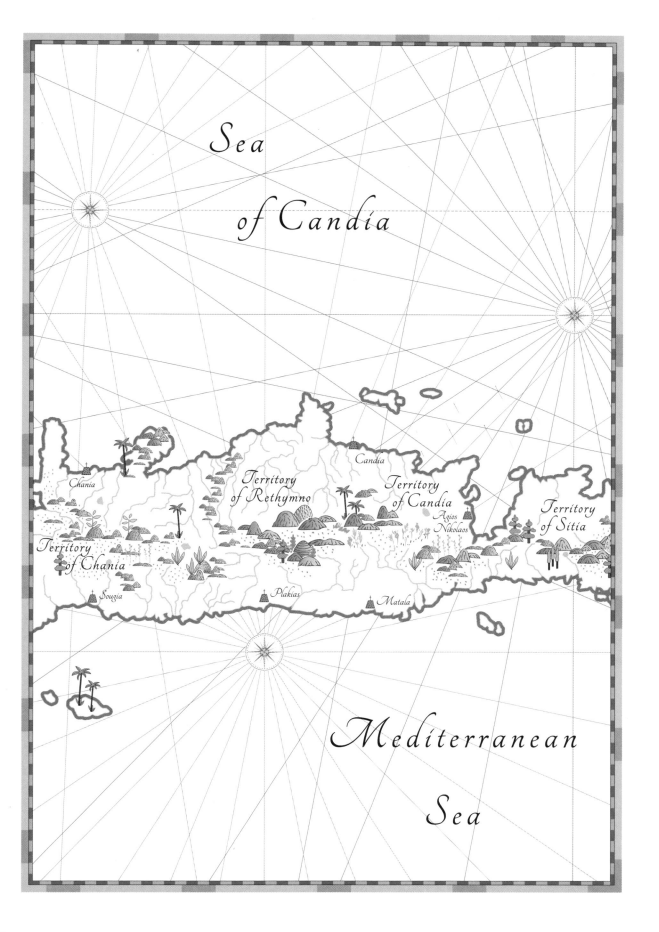

Sea

of Candia

Chania

Territory
of Rethymno

Candia

Territory
of Candia

Agios
Nikolaos

Territory
of Sitia

Territory
of Chania

Sougia

Plakias

Matala

Mediterranean

Sea

KYTHIRA

WITH THE MEDITERRANEAN WAVES lapping onto its west coast, and the Aegean Sea to its east, Kythira seems like a tiny isolated dot between the Peloponnese and Crete. Its sheer proportions contrast with the number of Greek myths that accompany its birth and have fed the imagination of Western writers and painters over the centuries. For the philosophers of antiquity—Hesiod, above all—it existed since the beginning of time. Remarkably, the ancient Greeks elected this little piece of land as the one to bear witness to the birth of the Titans and Aphrodite, the goddess of love.

Strollers on the Firi Ammos beach will be captivated by the splendor of the place and will understand what might have captured the imagination of the ancient Greeks. Gazing upon the azure sea hitting the red sand, they may envisage that a few miles offshore, the torrents are said to have engulfed the severed genitals of Uranus. And the fabulous beauty of the landscape could mingle in the walkers' minds with the appearance of Aphrodite, in a symphony in which heaven, love, sea, blood, and seed re-create a myth a thousand times written, a thousand times conveyed, a thousand times retold. The meeting point between the giants Uranus, Chronos, and Gaia, a land where heaven, Earth, and time converge, Kythira will forever be associated in humankind's dreams with being the chosen island where Aphrodite set her bare feet.

To celebrate this divine birth, the island's inhabitants erected a temple in honor of Aphrodite and founded a cult. In his *Histories*, Herodotus makes mention of the temple's existence and attributed its construction to the Phoenicians. In the Roman tradition, the island, associated with the goddess Venus, would for centuries remain the island of love and desire. Classical French painters and writers have entered into creative jousting tournaments to pass on to future generations the tempestuous fantasies associated with Kythira. *The Embarkation for Cythera* by French painter Jean-Antoine Watteau hides nothing in terms of the reported splendor of the island, and the beauty of the myth's women. What remains is the desire to love, the ultimate fantasy that will have its temple in Kythira, for the rest of time.

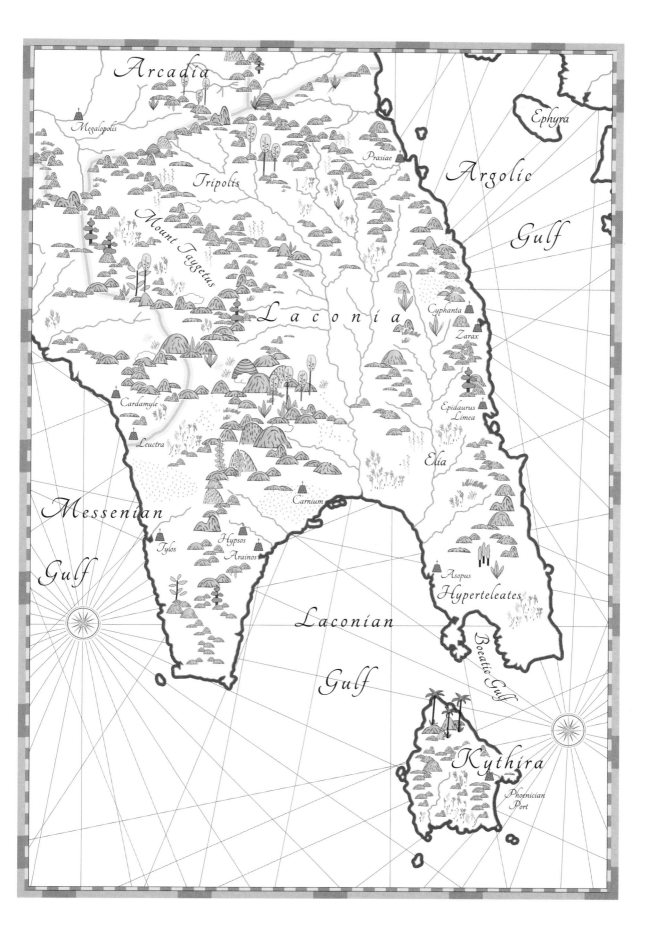

OGYGIA

DESTINY SEEMS TO HAVE elected certain places to protect them forever from the presence of human beings. Indeed, over the centuries, no one seems to have stayed on the island of Ogygia except Ulysses and the beautiful Calypso. When the hero arrived on the island where the nymph lived, the daughter of Atlas, he did not yet know that he would be staying there for seven years. Jan Brueghel the Elder has left behind a painting of this very scene in the *Odyssey* that suggests what this island may represent in the imagination of artists. Calypso gives in to Ulysses's embrace in a composition of shades of gold and green. The ineffable blue that pierces through the opening to the cave where the nymph lives gives the ensemble a majestic aura and a softness that chimes with the love that unites the two lovers. "There is no immortal whose eyes cannot be enthralled, whose soul cannot be enchanted," sang Homer.

Locating this island is another matter and still puzzles the experts. If Homer is to be believed, its vegetation could be that of the Moroccan coast. Herodotus locates it on the African coast along the Strait of Gibraltar. If we believe these assumptions, we must abandon the idea that Ogygia is an island. Everyone will put their own idea forward. And since Ogygie is described as an island of the Occident, why not consider the island of Gozo in the Maltese archipelago as a contender? Like Ogygia, Gozo is punctuated with caves and crevices. And its vegetation is similar to that described by Homer. According to Victor Bérard, author of the beautiful literary journey *Les Navigations d'Ulysse* [*Ulysses's Navigations*], Ogygia and Perejil Island are one and the same. His hypothesis is attractive indeed: Perejil has a rocky inlet sufficiently deep and wide for a boat to dock. Its waterfalls and forests of tall cedars and alders match Homer's descriptions. Located off the northern tip of the Moroccan coasts, it is detectable only by sailors who know the local waters. The perfect place for Calypso, whose name means "hidden." Beyond these guesses, a grain of doubt remains. As if, in the depths of one's self, we wanted to keep secret, for eternity, this place where the most beautiful of the nymphs lived, to preserve her den, forever invisible to the eyes of men—the den of our hearts.

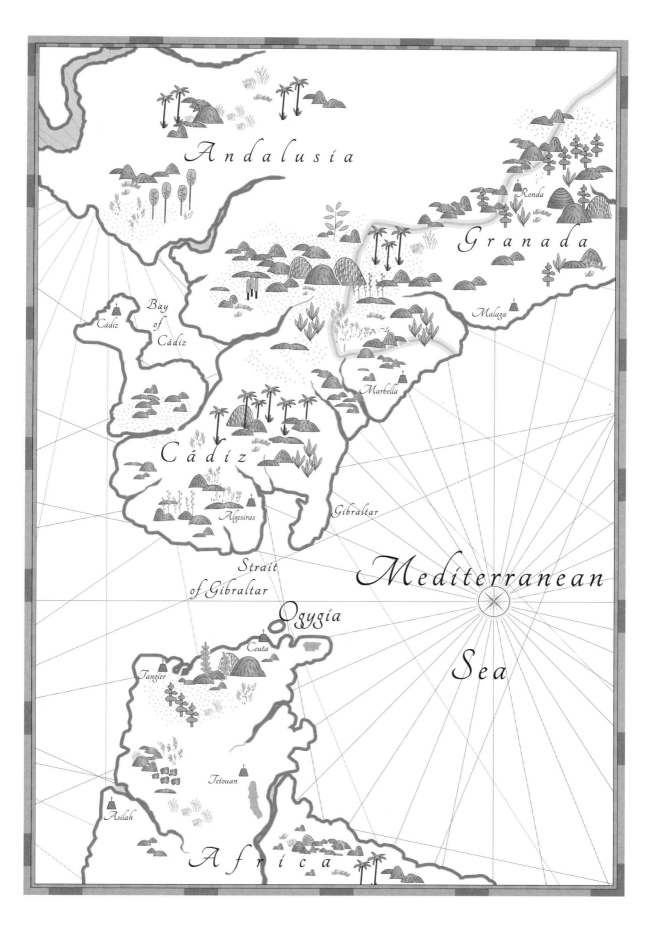

TROY

Priam's Treasure

EVEN IF ANCIENT MYTHS lend themselves to daydreaming, people in the modern era have often been committed to looking beyond those accounts to seek evidence that makes these beautiful legends a little more real.

When Heinrich Schliemann discovered the first remains of an ancient fortress at the site of Hisarlik in 1870, he was certain to have discovered Troy, whose memory had haunted the West for two millennia. The French traveler Marie-Gabriel-Florent-Auguste de Choiseul-Gouffier, assisted by Jean-Baptiste Le Chevalier, had already declared in 1776 to have located the ruins of the city under a hill near Burnabashi. In 1801, two English archeologists, Edward Daniel Clarke and John Martin Cripps, located Troy on a hill rising near Hisarlik. Schliemann, guided by the few topographical details left by Clarke and Cripps a century earlier, explored the western part of Turkey, which had been void of clues. The landscape consists of peaceful countryside. A few coppices of eucalyptus and olive trees line the vineyards under a burning sun. The Aegean Sea is not far away, nor are the Dardanelles, both at most a two-hour walk away. The silence imbues this site with a serenity that makes it difficult to recall battles, bloodshed, and fires. Schliemann discovered several strata of remains buried over time. Daydreaming took over his scientific mind when he stumbled across a stunning treasure. Gold jewelry, earrings, bracelets, rings, and brooches convinced Schliemann that he had found the jewels of the beautiful Helen of Troy. There was no doubt in his mind: he had exhumed King Priam's fabulous treasure. Schliemann hid his extraordinary find from the authorities. But he would eventually have to return his loot. It does not matter that further discoveries would refute his hypothesis: Schliemann had revived the mythical Troy along with its heroes.

Darda, Tros, Ilion . . . before becoming known as Troy, the mythical city would change its name several times—as well as its location on the maps of the world, before finding a fixed abode in Asia Minor, not far from the Aegean Sea, at the entrance of the Hellespont (now the Dardanelles). Troy, the mythical city cursed by fate after its sovereign, King Laomedon,

18

neglected to reward the gods Apollo and Poseidon for helping him fortify his city with thick tall walls. Troy, the warrior city, attacked and besieged, would fall in the twelfth century BCE in a mythical war against the Achaeans. In a war that lasted ten long years, as the aoidos Homer recounts in the *Iliad*, the famous poem of Ilion.

In the classical age and the Age of the Enlightenment, there were many travelers who—as readers of the Iliad and the Odyssey, dreaming, like Ulysses, of "making a fine journey"—would travel the length and breadth of the region of Troy, hoping to discover the walls and treasures of the mythical city.

Although destroyed, Troy continues to fascinate, and many are the epics that celebrate with pomp the descendants of Trojan heroes and the city's survivors. Far from stemming the tide of artistic imagination, the discovery of the city's presumed location gave new life to the heroes who had disappeared along with it. Hovering over the piles of stones, one can vividly imagine the ghosts of Paris and Helen, whose kidnapping unleashed the fury of the Achaeans. And who would not like to dream up Priam, Andromache, and Cassandra, perched on the remains of a rampart covered with wild herbs? Archeologists have provided proof that the city was destroyed by fire several times. In its ashes, one would have liked to find the remains of the wooden horse that Agamemnon brought into the fortress, and that would eventually mean the death of the city's inhabitants.

Over the centuries, writers have represented Troy as the most respected of civilizations. To ensure that even more grandeur and nobility would be bestowed upon the birth of Rome, Virgil, in his *Aeneid*, invented the city's Trojan roots. A millennium later, Benoît de Sainte-Maure composed *Le Roman de Troie* (*The Romance of Troy*), a monumental history of the prestigious city. In it, the chronicler refuses to allow the Trojan War to be a legend. Following in the vein of Dares Phrygius and Dictys Cretensis, he describes a glamorous Troy and the Trojans as a people of refined manners.

In the classical age and the Age of the Enlightenment, there were many travelers who—as readers of the *Iliad* and the *Odyssey*, dreaming, like Ulysses, of "making a fine journey"—would travel the length and breadth of the region of Troy, hoping to discover the walls and treasures of the mythical city. Centuries have erased the atrocities committed by the Achaeans, leaving behind nothing but the memory of exploits and deadly liaisons. Men and gods have once again taken possession of the people's imagination. And even if modern-day historians have demonstrated that all that took place at Troy was a brawl between a few groups of men with brutal manners, it is still nice to imagine Athena racing to the rescue of Achilles, among soaring javelins, bull-skin shields, and glittering armor as blinding as the sun. Too bad if Hector's corpse, tied to the back of Achilles' chariot, left a streak of blood around the walls that made Andromache faint. Too bad if the bones of his young son Astyanax, thrown from the top of the city walls, would be piled onto the many corpses peppering the plains. The passing years quickly erased the memories of horror. And the ruins of Troy, set among vineyards, offer visitors nothing but yet another opportunity to perpetuate the magic of legends.

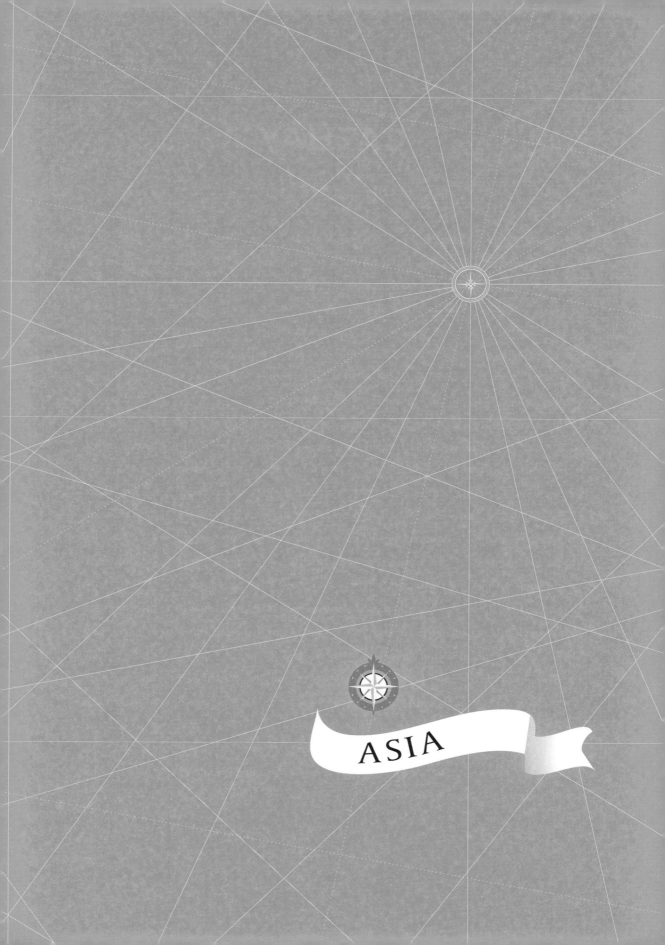

ASIA

CATHAY

On the Edge of Paradise

SINCE ANTIQUITY, the Far East has been famous for the beauty of its silk. In their writings, both Pliny the Elder and Seneca called the region the "land of the Seres." In the Middle Ages, travelers on Mongolian roads entered an area whose inhabitants called themselves the Khitan people, or the Kitai: the name "Cathay" developed from this ethnonym, to refer to the people's territory, which corresponds roughly to modern-day China. At the time, geographers, cartographers, and cosmographers agreed on locating paradise on Earth in northern Asia. Faithful to biblical tradition, they readily placed the lands of Gog and Magog there. This part of the world fascinates people. Some scholars even think that the Great Khan and Prester John were in fact one and the same person.

During his voyage through Asia in 1254, William of Rubruck, a Franciscan monk of Flemish origin, encountered very different peoples. Uighurs, Tanguts, and Tibetans of the North give him the opportunity for short but picturesque descriptions. If Tibetans are described as "very strong men," Koreans are "small people, swarthy like the Spaniards" (translated by Peter Jackson). Twenty years before Marco Polo, he painted the first portrait of Chinese people as "small men, who in speaking aspirate strongly through the nose, and in common with all Orientals, have small openings for the eyes," he observes. The mood of the time made him refer to Prester John, but he says, "Though when I passed through his pasture lands, no one knew anything of him."

At the turn from the twelfth to the thirteenth century, Giovanni di Montecorvino, another Franciscan monk from Puglia, stayed in Armenia and Persia before traveling to Mongolian China in the company of a Black Friar, Nicola de Pistra, and a merchant, Pietro de Lucalongo. He spoke the language of Tartary. Having discovered Cathay, he lived there for forty years, an eternity for the era. . . . However, it was due to Marco Polo's accounts that, in far-off places, Cathay would rise to the rank of a mythical land. In the *Travels of Marco Polo*, Rustichello da Pisa, who was Marco Polo's secretary in a way, writes: "For I would have you to know that, from the creation of Adam to the present day, no Pagan, or Saracen, or Christian, or any other person of whatever race or generation, explored so many parts of the world or saw such great wonders as this Messer Marco Polo" (translated by Hugh Murray).

Marco Polo had a penchant for exaggeration. He is ecstatic about the Great Khan's palace, which can be dismantled, and the golden roofs of its pagodas, which Christopher Columbus would take for palaces, and that he would search in vain on the islands of the West Indies.

Referring to the Yellow Sea, Marco Polo notes that it is so long and wide that "according to skillful and intelligent mariners who have made the voyage, it contains 7,448 isles, mostly inhabited."

Marco Polo not only sought wonders; he also brought some back with him. When Marco returned to Venice with his father, Niccolò, and his uncle Maffeo in 1295, few would believe that the same men had left twenty-four years earlier. They brought back fabulous stories from their voyages to Cathay, Cipangu, and India. And to convince even the most incredulous, they removed from their coat lining gems, pearls, and diamonds they brought with them, as well as precious relics from these lands at the end of the world. Some remained skeptical.

When Marco Polo was on his deathbed in 1323, Jacopo de Cequi confessed to him that he thought "there were many strange things in his book and that they defied credulity." The traveler retorted that he had not revealed "half of what he had actually seen."

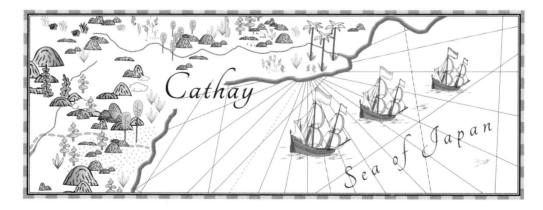

The West's fascination with Cathay was not diminished by the publication of Marco Polo's travels—on the contrary. Niccolò and Maffeo Polo's exploration of China, followed by Marco's, were probably the first of the Age of Discovery, long before the "discovery" of America. Cathay would never stop to fascinate people. And Columbus would never have "discovered" America—according to legend—had he not tried to find a passage to India, Cipangu, and Cathay, taking a westerly route.

Although he did not find the golden palaces described by Marco Polo on either of his first two trips, Columbus never doubted having reached India. He estimated that Cathay and Cipangu were not far apart from each other. It was only on his third voyage that he changed his mind. But it was too late: his gold rush had already spread to many of his peers. And the fact that the land they were exploring was not the mythical Cathay, the legendary Cipangu, or the fabulous Indies mattered very little to Francisco Pizarro or Francisco de Orellana. Other myths about gold had taken their place and animated their dreams of conquests and glory: the legends of Paititi, El Dorado, and the Seven Cities of Gold.

> To convince even the most incredulous, they removed from their coat lining gems they brought with them, as well as precious relics from these lands at the end of the world.

CIPANGU

The Archipelago in the Levant

EARLY ON, Marco Polo's dreamland Cipangu would lose its beautiful name "Land of the Rising Sun," which the Venetian had translated from the Chinese. Since the discovery of the island by the Portuguese in the sixteenth century, it would become known as Giapan. Soon, Cipangu—like India and Cathay—would represent in the collective imagination of the West the most fabulous aspects of the East and thus feed the dreams and fantasies of travelers, merchants, cartographers, and people of letters alike. Marco Polo had dreamed it up: the description he gave of it was a secondhand account—he had never actually reached the island. Two centuries later, Christopher Columbus, who thought he was traversing the archipelago, in his wild idea of finding a passage west to India, found a continent instead of an island—and we all know which one that was! The thirteenth-century Western travelers William of Rubruck and Giovanni di Pian Carpino traveled across the Near and Middle East, crossing the vastness of Tartary. Odoric de Pordenone even reached Borneo and described the local cannibal tribes armed with poisoned arrows. But none of them reached the island of Cipangu. One of the first Europeans to describe the archipelago, which happened to look like an arc, was Marco Polo. In his *Book of the Marvels of the World*, he makes mention of this island he would never reach: "But first, I must mention the many isles in this sea lying to the eastward; and first, one named Zipangu. This is a very large island, 1,500 miles from the continent. The people are fair, handsome, and of agreeable manners. They are idolaters and live quite separate, entirely independent of all other nations. Gold is very abundant, and no man being allowed to export it, while no merchant goes thence to the mainland, the people accumulate a vast amount" (translated by Hugh Murray). He continues: "But I will give you a wonderful account of a very large palace, all covered with that metal, as our churches are with lead. It is of such a value that one can scarcely imagine. The pavement of the chamber, the halls, windows, and every other part, have it laid on 2 inches thick, so that the riches of this palace are incalculable. Here are also

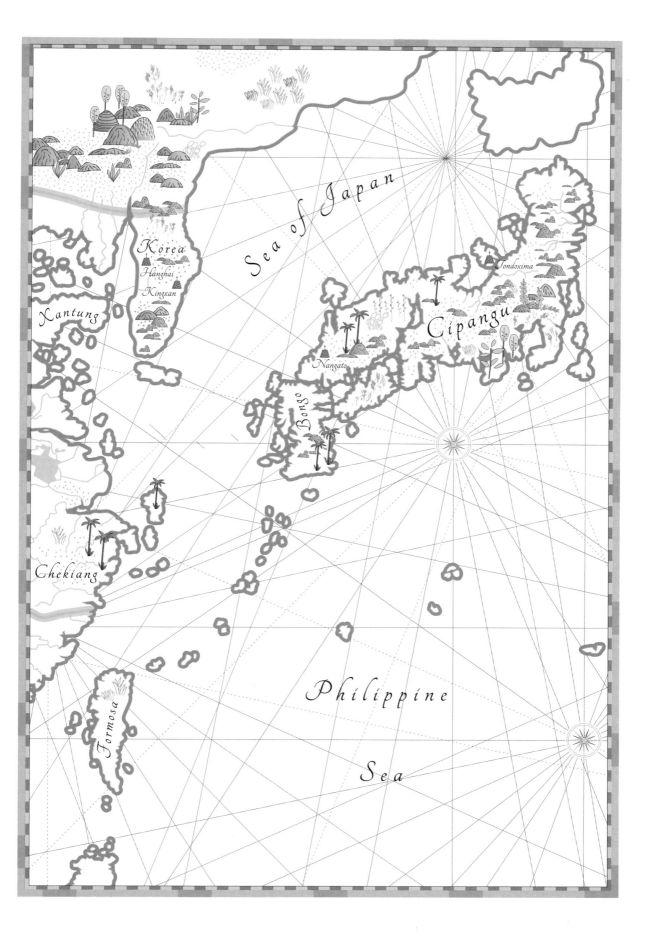

red pearls, large, and of equal value with the white, with many other precious stones. Kublai, on hearing of this amazing wealth, desired to conquer the island." (translated by Hugh Murray).

When he set sail from Palos de la Frontera, along the Rio Tinto in Andalusia, on August 3, 1492, Columbus was haunted by the idea of opening a new passage to reach India, Cathay, and Cipangu going west: his aim was to ransack their extraordinary treasures. So when he reached the West Indies, passing from San Salvador to Haiti via Cuba, he was convinced that he had found India and was just a few days' sailing away from Cathay and Cipangu. His conviction was as much distorted by miscalculations as it was by the faith in Marco Polo's accounts. Upon discovering a lush landscape and encountering Indigenous peoples that were just as affable as the Venetian had described two centuries earlier, he did not yet know that his geographical location was wrong: the latitude noted on his parchments had not taken the North Star as its reference point. So one could say that the true star guiding Christopher Columbus was in fact Marco Polo. He was not the only one. Following the example of the German cartographer Martin Behaim, many reckoned that "Ptolemy did not describe the world any farther [than the Ganges], but Marco Polo did."

> Cipangu would represent in the collective imagination of the West the most fabulous aspects of the East and thus feed the dreams and fantasies of travelers, merchants, and cartographers.

Legend has it that it was at the end of his third journey that Christopher Columbus, amazed at the dimensions of the Parias Peninsula, finally understood that this land could not be an island. He was not off the coast of Cipangu, but on the threshold of an unknown continent that posed an unavoidable obstacle on the road to India. . . . Cosmographers and cartographers would concur with this hypothesis: they would draw a land of uncertain contours to the west, and, to the east, India, from Cathay to Cipangu.

A new layout of continents and islands on globes and maps of the world would gradually emerge, with Asia on the right and the new continent America on the left. It gave cartographers the perfect opportunity to avoid the question of what void it was that was separating Cathay and Cipangu from these newly discovered lands. It worked so well, in fact, that at the dawn of the sixteenth century, the question of the distance between the newly discovered lands and India, Cathay, and Cipangu remained unresolved. Giovanni Matteo Contarini, in his attempt to synthesize the existing knowledge, placed the West Indies not far from Cipangu on his map, while Martín Fernández de Enciso perpetuated the existing confusion over this unknown part of the globe by adding the distances established by Ptolemy in degrees, and routes instead of leagues. His map of the world is a sum of errors: he took Cathay for Mangi, mixed up Java and Sumatra, and Champa with Cipangu. In 1566, on Bolognino Zaltieri's map, Cipangu became Giapan.

The archipelago's coastline, like that of the Taprobana coast, took on a more precise shape thanks to reports by Portuguese navigators, who set foot on the island in 1543. However, the geography of the coast and island of these parts of the world would remain very approximate until the late sixteenth century. And it was not until the beginning of the following century that Luis Teixeira would provide the first fairly reliable map of the isles of Japan.

COLCHIS

NO ONE RECOGNIZES the name "Colchis" anymore. Centuries have erased the moniker, with its sweet ring, from humankind's collective memory. The only reminder is the Latin name *Colchicum autumnale*, for a little flower that blooms at the end of August and is abundant in Asia Minor, and particularly in Georgia, on the eastern shore of the Black Sea: the autumn crocus. Colchis would have most definitely been erased from the imagination of humankind, had it not been the land of the Golden Fleece of which the ancient Greeks sang. Who hasn't heard of the adventure of Jason and the Argonauts? Two thousand years ago, Colchis was considered one of the limits of the ecumene, the known world. The Black Sea, called the Euxine Sea then, was the subject of terrifying legends. To reach the eastern shore of the Euxine Sea, one had to pass through a strait flanked by cliffs that clashed together whenever a vessel went through: the Symplegades.

Let's recall: tyrannized by their stepmother Ino, King Athamas's son Phrixus and daughter Helle implore Zeus to rescue them. The god of gods then sends them Chrysomallos, a powerful winged ram with golden wool and horns. Straddling the animal immediately, the two teenagers flee. But as they are flying over the ocean, Helle falls off and drowns at the mouth of the Euxine Sea: the Hellespont (now the Dardanelles) would be named after her. So Phrixus finally arrives at Colchis on his own, where he sacrifices the ram in honor of Zeus before giving the Golden Fleece to King Aeëtes. There are multiple variations of this myth. Depending on the source, the Golden Fleece is suspended from the branches of an oak tree or hidden in a cave guarded by a dragon. This is where the famous Jason enters the scene, whose name has been passed down to posterity, and who has inspired painters, playwrights, and filmmakers. Sent by his uncle Pelias, king of Iolcus in Thessaly, he went to Colchis on the quest for the Golden Fleece. Several trials await him, set by Aeëtes. He masters each one of them thanks to the help of the king's burning daughter, the sorceress Medea, who has succumbed to Jason's charms and harbors an all-consuming passion for him. The Fleece retrieved, Medea joins Jason and the

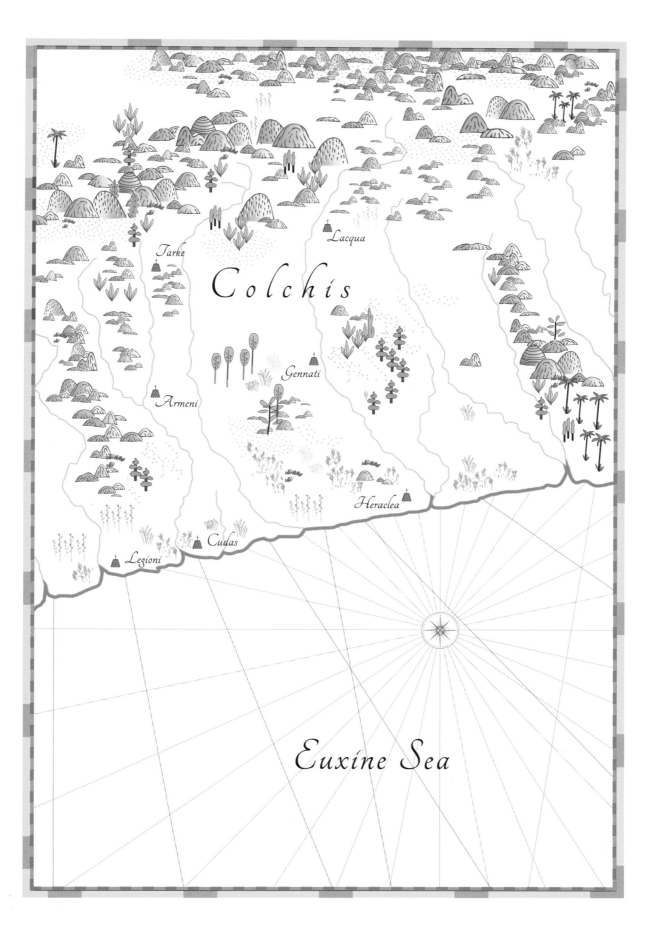

Argonauts on board the Argo and flees Colchis, where, as a traitor to her own father, she is no longer welcome. However, the crew cannot enjoy their victory for long: the men will perish, as Seneca explains, "atoned for the sea's outraged laws" (translated by Frank Justus Miller). The fate of Jason and Medea is sealed. "O how I wish that ship the Argo | had never sailed off to the land of Colchis, | past the Symplegades, those dark dancing rocks | which smash boats sailing through the Hellespont. | I wish they'd never chopped the pine trees down | in those mountain forests up on Pelion, | to make oars for the hands of those great men who set off, on Pelias's orders, | to fetch the

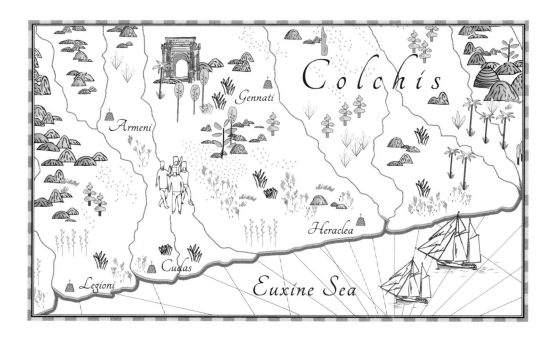

golden fleece," laments the Nurse in Euripides's Medea (translated by Ian Johnston). "Then my mistress, | Medea, never would have sailed away | to the towers in the land of Iolcus, | her heart passionately in love with Jason. | She'd never have convinced those women, | Pelias' daughters, to kill their father, | and she'd not have come to live in Corinth | with her husband and her children—well loved | in exile by those whose land she'd moved to."

For a long time, the geographical location of Colchis and the origin of its people were subjected to the whims of historians. Although we know today that this mythical land is located in the heart of Georgia, and that its population is Caucasian, Herodotus considered them of Egyptian origin: he purported to have come across tanned people with frizzy hair in this country. He attributed their presence to a colony founded by King Sesostris. This hypothesis enticed many others—Voltaire being one of them! In the seventeenth century, Lambertini and Chardin would leave these strange interpretations aside, preferring to stick instead to the story of Jason and the Golden Fleece. One way to recognize whether a myth is the product of fantasy is that the latter contains more kernels of truth than any apparently rational explanations—especially when these constructs mumble something that tends to make these lands appear even more foreign than the myths that have engendered them.

To reach Colchis, at the edge of the known world, one had to pass through a strait flanked by cliffs that clashed together whenever a vessel went through: the Symplegades.

THE MUGHAL EMPIRE

A Land of Wonder

"IT IS THE MOST BEAUTIFUL and magnificent country in the world." That is how Marco Polo described, in very few words, his impressions upon discovering India. This is important news to the medieval world, and perhaps as surprising for its civilization as the first steps on the moon were for us. India is the object of fascinating descriptions. In addition to the gold, which is apparently found there in abundance, its fauna and inhabitants seek their match in the known world. In antiquity, the most-extravagant assumptions were coming thick and fast. According to Herodotus, animals there were smaller than ours; according to Pliny, they were monstrous in size. As for the trees, their height made their canopies inaccessible to soaring arrows. Pliny mentions fig trees that had grown to the size of a "cavalry squadron." Ctesias is even more imaginative: the enormous mountains that are all over India are the home of baboon-like creatures. A millennium later, many medieval illuminations actually depicted men with the heads of dogs, dressed in white togas, bartering, or reading enigmatic books.

Until the Middle Ages, India was this vastness at the end of the earth, east where the sun rises. Its stifling heat was mentioned, conducive to nature's most astonishing excesses. Many fabulous animals, phoenixes and unicorns, baboons, and one-footed monopods had apparently evolved in these fantastical lands rich in precious stones.

In the thirteenth century, William of Rubruck visited Asia. When he met a delegation sent by the Great Khan, he tried to find out about this country of which so little was known. He was told to go farther west. Rubruck traveled with this delegation for three weeks, without success. His peer, the Franciscan monk Giovanni di Montecorvino, would have better luck: he was to have the coveted privilege of providing the first description of the inhabitants of this strange country, "as I have seen and in particular noted with my own eyes" (translated by Colonel Sir Henry Yule). He said about the Indigenous people of the Malabar Coast, where he had just arrived from the southwest of the peninsula: "They are not, strictly speaking, black, but of an olive colour, and exceedingly well formed both women and men. They go barefoot and naked, except that they wear a cloth round the loins. . . . They shave not the beard; many times a day they wash."

Strictly speaking, India was part of the Mughal Empire for only two centuries, from 1500 to 1700, when it had been conquered by the Muslim Turko-Mongols. Marco Polo preceded this invasion, which brought about notable changes in people's habits, by two centuries. When he arrived in India, he was dazzled by the magnificence of this people's religious practices. This was long before it became seeped in Persian culture with the arrival of Timur, two centuries later, which resulted in the emergence of a religion combining elements of Islam and Brahmanism. Marco Polo did not get to observe the effects of the sharia on local customs. As a close friend of Kublai Khan, the grandson of the great Genghis Khan, he was very familiar with Mongolian customs. India is fascinating. It is considered a paradise on Earth. Some say Noah's ark ran aground here. And in Western traditions, it is referred to as the country of origin of the Three Magi. Marco Polo's tales of pearl fishing depict a peaceful and calm civilization, averse to war, and that when it comes to conflict, employed mercenaries do the dirty work. And if any sea monsters threatened fishermen, priests' prayers were enough to chase them off. In the imagination of the Renaissance, the people of India were associated with man in his original heavenly form. People there walked around naked, as did their kings, solely adorned with precious stones whose brilliance added to the majesty of their surroundings. The animals described by Marco Polo are commensurate with wonders: "Such as a black lion, without either spot or mark; parrots of numerous kinds, some white as snow, with red beak and feet; others red and white, most lovely; and some extremely small, and also very beautiful. The peacocks are much larger, handsomer, and of a different species from ours. . . . In short, they have all things, fruits, beasts, and birds, dissimilar to ours, and both handsomer and better " (translated by Hugh Murray). Marco Polo also mentions

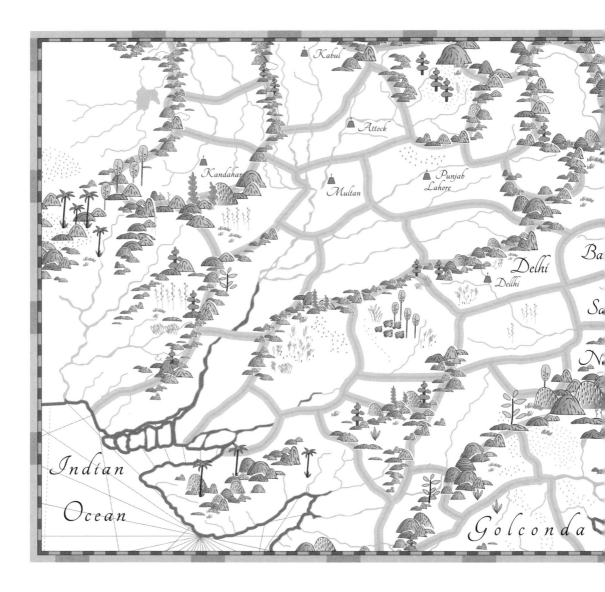

the fabulous quantities of pepper, ginger, cotton, and indigo found in the province of Gujarat. When the Arab traveler Ibn Battuta would visit India on his journey, he would add nothing new to the stories told by Rubruck, Montecorvino, and Marco Polo.

Christopher Columbus, animated by the prospect of opening up a new commercial route by reach-

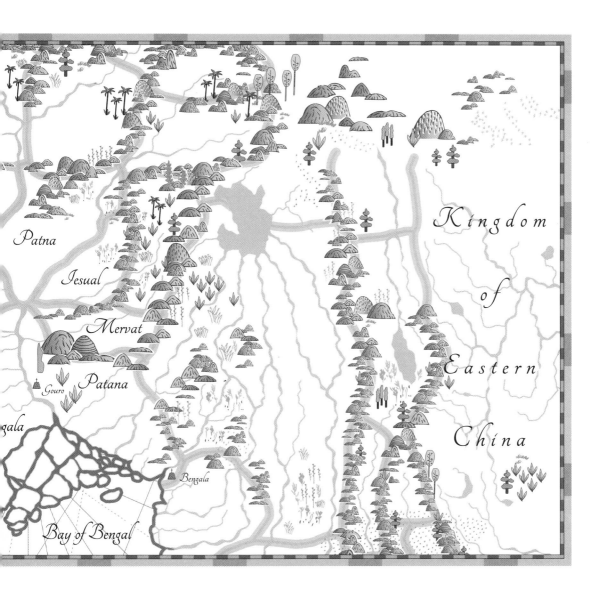

Patna

Iesual

Mervat

Gouro *Patana*

gala

Bengala

Bay of Bengal

Kingdom

of

Eastern

China

ing the famous India going west, implored Queen Isabella I of Castile to grant him command of a fleet. Although the Genoese would not discover India, he was so captured by the enduring desire that has haunted Western minds since antiquity that he would remain deeply attached to his conviction that it was indeed the fabulous Indies he had discovered on his first journey.

GOLCONDA

The Kingdom of the Blessed

TOWERING MORE THAN 330 feet above the plains of Telangana in the heart of India, the remains of the fortified city of Golconda are the last witnesses of an ephemeral kingdom whose capital it was from the fourteenth to the early sixteenth centuries. The earliest fortress was built here in the mid-twelfth century by the Hindu Kakatiya dynasty. It then became the emblem of a sophisticated civilization. Ahmednagar and Bidara formed the state of Deccan. The Turkmen governor of the Bahmani Sultanate founded the Qutb Shahi dynasty, which would run the city and the Sultanate of Golconda for nearly a century. Under this dynasty, important works on the expansion and defensive structure of the fortress were carried out. Brick stones were replaced with granite. A huge stone wall was erected around the stronghold to protect it from possible attacks. At the end of the sixteenth century, Golconda was no longer the capital, but it continued to prosper thanks to its diamond mines, celebrating the sophistication of its inhabitants and their art of delicate miniature painting. This opulence would arouse envy: the Mughal emperor Aurangzeb besieged the fortress for eight months before a traitor allowed him to enter the city triumphantly. Aurangzeb left the proud Golconda in ruins, leaving intact only the Fateh Darwaza, the "Victory Gate," and a few other buildings. But Golconda would survive in the Western imagination. Driven by the so-called orientalist wave set in motion by the first translation of the *Arabian Nights*, Golconda would fuel the creativity of Enlightenment writers. In Stanislas de Boufflers's story *The Queen of Golconda*, the narrator describes his stay there: "I traveled through different kingdoms that share this vast country [India], and I stopped in Golconda; it was then the most flourishing state in Asia. The people were happy under the reign of a woman who ruled over the king with her beauty, and the kingdom with her wisdom." A prosperous kingdom where peasants cultivated land for themselves and the treasurers did not collect taxes for their own benefit. During the Enlightenment, Golconda became a mythical, utopian kingdom that combined opulence with the gentleness of life under the auspices of a wise queen.

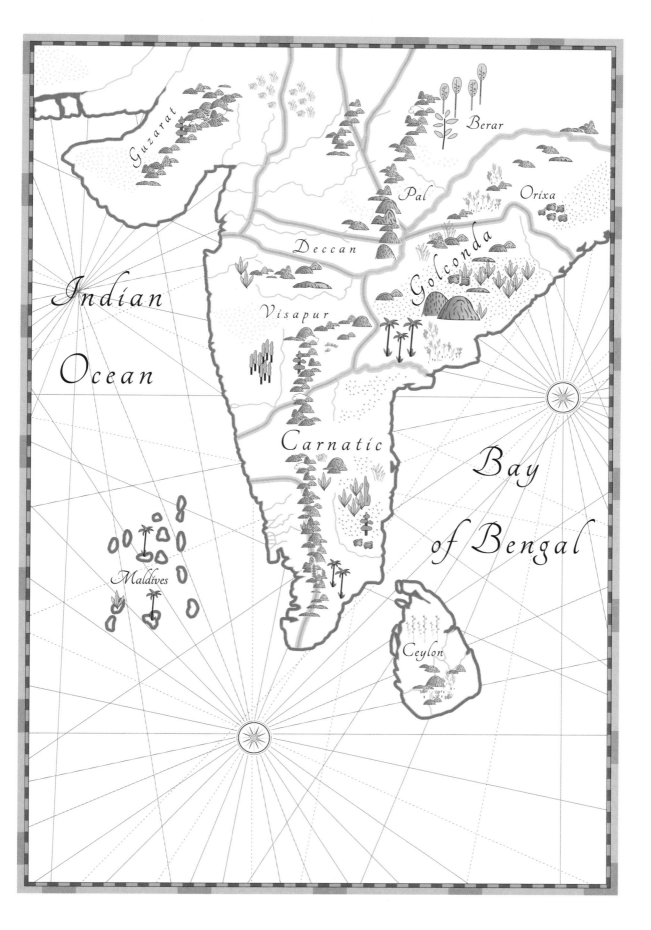

KAFIRISTAN

The Land of Kings

THE FOLLOWING SCENE is described in an anthology: in the office of the *Northern Star's* editor in chief, the former soldiers and Freemasons Peachey Carnehan and Daniel Dravot are signing a contract to become kings of Kafiristan, vouching to deny themselves alcohol and women and to remain loyal to each other. Dressed as merchants, they head for the road. Two years later, Carnehan, in tatters, reappeared in the same office to recount his terrible adventure. Yes, he and Dravot had reached Kafiristan, and they had become the kings of the land.

Immortalized on the silver screen by Sean Connery and Michael Caine, Rudyard Kipling's novella *The Man Who Would Be King* made the country at the edge of India known to the wider public—a land that Alexander the Great had crossed once, but that no other European had reached since.

In this novella, Kipling, who liked to believe in the existence of Kafiristan, deployed a treasure trove of imagination with unparalleled virtuosity, blending the legend with the haughtiest ideas of the British Empire. Arrived at their destination, his two heroes unite the tribes, arm them, and fight alongside them. An arrow hits Dravot, piercing the leather of his cartridge belt without hurting him—so the natives regard the two strangers as either gods or devils. They thus submit to them.

The two friends could have stayed and died as kings if Dravot, wanting to found an empire and a dynasty, had not decided to take a wife. "How can daughters of men marry gods or devils?" the kingdom's priests and high dignitaries asked. The chosen future wife gives Dravot a kiss in the presence of priests and the people, then she bites him. He starts to bleed, and the fraud is uncovered. "Neither god nor devil but a man!" scream the priests. The two kings are ruthlessly prosecuted. Dravot's reign ended for him at the bottom of a ravine, while Peachey was crucified but survived.

Returning to the office of the very editor in chief who had welcomed them before their wild escapade, Peachey lays before him Dravot's head wrapped in a linen cloth—the only testimony of their adventure.

Readers of the time knew that the fabulous Indies depicted by Marco Polo were miles off the real India. But they continued to be fascinated by it and coveted it. In the days of Empress Victoria, Britain not only hoisted all its sails out on the oceans; it extended its dominance over newly discovered continents and lands as well. While Australia was reserved for deportees and convicts and became its largest jail, the fast-paced metropolises of India—Delhi, Calcutta, and Bombay—were the jewels in the crown of the empire. In their novels, Joseph Conrad and Rudyard Kipling would not cease to elaborate on its charms and splendors while praising the greatness of the British Empire. But India still fascinated people, notably the well-educated traveler Kipling, because a part of the country's hinterland, in the almost unexplored mountain regions, remained virtually unknown. This is the breeding ground that continues to nurture fantasies, myths, and legends, as Kipling's novella shows.

India still fascinated people, notably travelers such as Kipling and Conrad, because a part of the country's hinterland, in the almost unexplored mountain regions, remained virtually unknown.

Empire

Turkestan

Chinese

Empire

...khara

Kafiristan

...stan

Kashmir

India

THE LAND OF THE CIMMERIENS

A Land of Mist and Darkness

SOME ACCOUNTS HAVE PLUNGED into the dark past of centuries ago, never to reappear. Others have been obstinately inspiring the imagination of our contemporaries. Ancient myths, British fantasies, video games, and movies have made these barbarian heroes, dreaded warriors, half men, and half gods familiar, these characters that are somewhere between good and evil, ready to avenge, destroy, repair, and annihilate. It was probably this particular people's closeness to hell that has inspired so many poets. Let's look at Homer again: The sorceress Circe invites Ulysses to enter Hades, where Tiresias will reveal to him the road to follow to return to Ithaca. In the *Odyssey*, the road to the land of the dead passes through the land of the Cimmerians. That indicates how closely this people has been associated with Hades for millennia. The historians of antiquity locate this terrible people around the current Sea of Azov. Ovid, in his *Metamorphoses*, describes this area as invaded by mist and darkness. "To that dark cave | the Sun, when rising or in middle skies, | or setting, never can approach with light. | There dense fogs, mingled with the dark, exhale | darkness from the black soil" (translated by Brookes More). This tradition, passed on through engravings and paintings of the Romantic era, while being shrouded in impenetrable mist, inspired almost entirely the imagination of composers Richard Wagner, Franz Liszt, and Alexander Borodine. One constant remains, however: the connection between the land of the Cimmerians and shadows and, by analogy, clouds, mist, and fog. As a result, people of antiquity frequently located it, like the Garden of the Hesperides, in the Far West, in Tauris, or in places that were suspected of having links with Hades. In his *Histories*, Herodotus reports that the Cimmerians were subjected to the law of the Scythians, and that, forced to abandon their homeland, they had to wander, like lost souls, before finding refuge on the shores of the Black Sea. Strabo turns the Cimmerians into people living in subterranean worlds, waiting for night to fall to risk venturing outside, and thus reconnects with the rich Homeric imagination that makes them a people of the shadows and the night.

TAPROBANA

End of the World

TAPROBANA . . . it is by this enchanting name that the island of Sri Lanka was first known. Whether it derived from the Sanskrit word *tamraparni*, for "copper-colored leaf," or from the Sinhalese *tambapanni*, for "red hands," it evokes both the shape of the island and the earthy color of its land molded by its first inhabitants, who originated from the foothills of northern India.

In antiquity, the story went that Egyptians had traveled there in twenty days aboard boats woven from papyrus leaves. For Greek navigators, this is the land at the end of the world, the "land of the Antichtones." In the fourth century BCE, Alexander the Great's fleet reached this island, which was known only from sailors' lore. A century later, Megasthenes claimed that the island possessed more gold and pearls than India, stoking the desire of Greek and Roman merchants. Pliny evoked the story of the freedman Annius Plocamus, who, having spent six months on the island, gave an enchanting description of it. In search of precious stones and gems, Ludovico di Varthema and the rich Venetians Cesare Federici and Gaspare Balbi visited the island and also advantageously stumbled upon other places on their journey whose names are evocative of dreams and wealth: Pegu, Bengal, Negapatam, Sumatra, Java, Champa, etc. But the lure of profit was not the only driver behind these enterprises: what was fascinating about Taprobana was also what it represented for many erudite travelers. Indeed, from the merchant Sulaiman al-Tajir's journey in the ninth century, to the later stories of Sinbad the Sailor's fabulous adventures, the stories agree that after the fall from paradise, Adam and Eve had found refuge here. As a result, many Christian authors, proudly supported and retold by the Indigenous population, have insisted on making Taprobana the location of paradise on Earth. In *A Relation of Some Yeares Travaile into Afrique* (1634), the English traveler Thomas Herbert jokes: "For it is apparent, that on the high peake (cald by the Europaeans) Columbo, tis orthodoxally held by them, that Adam was their Created and liued there, they beleeue it rather in regard his vestigatings are yet imprinted in the earth, but generally the Inhabitants are egregious Paynims." To this day, locals are proud to show travelers this footprint.

TARTARY

Land of the Devils

THERE ARE EMPIRES like glaciers covering mountainsides: they grow or shrink depending on the era. The one that the Middle Ages called Tartary stretched from the Urals to the Pacific Ocean in the thirteenth century. And if the term "Tartars" refers to the Mongolian people, their land extended beyond the borders of their current territory: Genghis Khan led them right up to Europe's doorstep. In the mid-thirteenth century, Christian civilizations anxiously and fearfully wondered about "this appalling breed of unholy men, of monsters that have nothing human about them."

In 1227, upon the death of Genghis Khan, his successors split this vast empire among them. The Mongolian hordes wreaked havoc and left a trail of destruction behind. The Tartars' vanguards were reported to have made it to the gates of Italy, sowing terror that was ten times worse than the fear of the unknown.

In 1245, Pope Innocent IV charged the Franciscan monk Giovanni da Pian del Carpine with a most delicate mission: to visit the Great Khan Güyük Khan to "examine all things carefully." It was in the Lower Volga region that the monk entered the territory of the Tartars. Despite some apprehension, he was convinced he would be bringing the Good News to the "barbarian nations." Giovanni was spared neither obstacles nor frights. Nevertheless, he would still be in close contact with his hosts—at least close enough to provide the following depiction in his *Ystoria Mongalorum*: "The Mongols or Tartars, in outward shape, are vnlike to all other people. For they are broader betweene the eyes, and the balles of their cheekes, then men of other nations bee. They haue flat and small noses, litle eyes, and eye liddes standing streight vpright. . . . They haue short feet also " (translated by Charles Raymond Beazley).

Between 1254 and 1255, Louis IX—the future Saint Louis—in turn, sent another delegation to the Great Khan, headed by the Flemish Franciscan monk William of Rubruck. The latter promised his sovereign: "I will write to you everything I have seen. I will describe to you their lives and manners as well as I can." He will keep his word: he will deliver a similar and equally eloquent description of the Tartars in his *Itinerarium*. Indeed, Saint Louis would have the opportunity to judge for himself the veracity of his envoy's descriptions. During the Seventh Crusade, he would receive the Khan's emissaries in Damietta, who had come to offer to him their help in liberating the tomb of Christ.

Marco Polo would eventually have the great privilege of removing the invisible border that had separated the medieval West from that empire at the end of the world. Once arrived at Kublai Khan's court, he would serve as his ambassador for seventeen years. Let us imagine this sophisticated Venetian, well accustomed to the manners of Italy already in the thrall of the Renaissance, learning the language of his hosts, adopting their clothes and customs, and shooting bow and arrow in a way that impressed the chronicler Rustichello da Pisa. Dictated by Marco Polo, the very Rustichello would write: "The wealthy wear rich robes of gold and silk, with varied furs of the ermine, sable, and fox. Their harness is beautiful and of great value" (translated by Hugh Murray). The horde's exotic pomp had influenced the Italian's habits: three centuries later, in 1556, Giovanni Battista Ramusio would note in his *Navigationi et Viaggi* that upon his return to Venice, Marco Polo looked like a Tartar himself, "his facial expression, his clothes, and his language." The discovery of this unknown world brought with it many wonders, as the prodigy Rustichello reports: "I will tell you, too, a great wonder which these baksi do by their enchantments. When the monarch sits at table in his hall of state, and the cups are ten paces distant, full of wine, milk, and other beverages, they cause them, by their magical spells, to rise from the pavement and place themselves before the prince, without any one touching them." Under the reign of the great Kublai Khan, Tartary certainly reached its peak. Never again would it achieve this level of sophistication and grandeur that had conquered the heart of Marco Polo, and subsequently those of his readers.

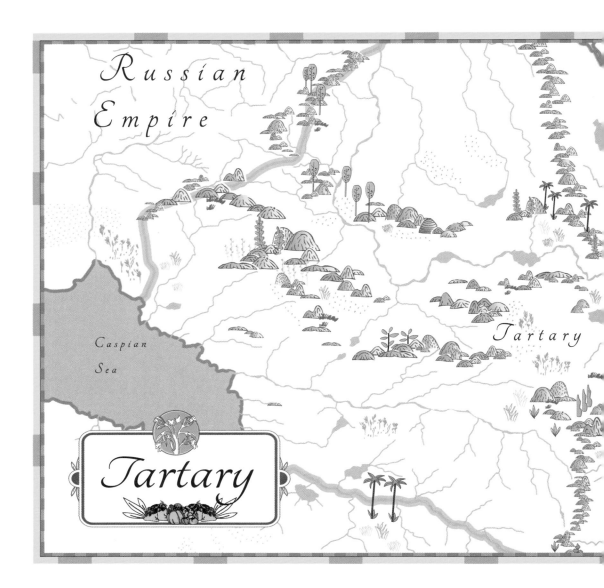

Russian Empire

Caspian Sea

Tartary

Tartary

At the beginning of the seventeenth century, Tartary extended from the eastern part of Poland to the Far East, and from the Caspian Sea to the Arctic Ocean. Unlike Muscovy, of which the traveler Sigismund von Herberstein gave a rich description in the previous century, Tartary was still a little-known land. Most of the sources stem from Marco Po-

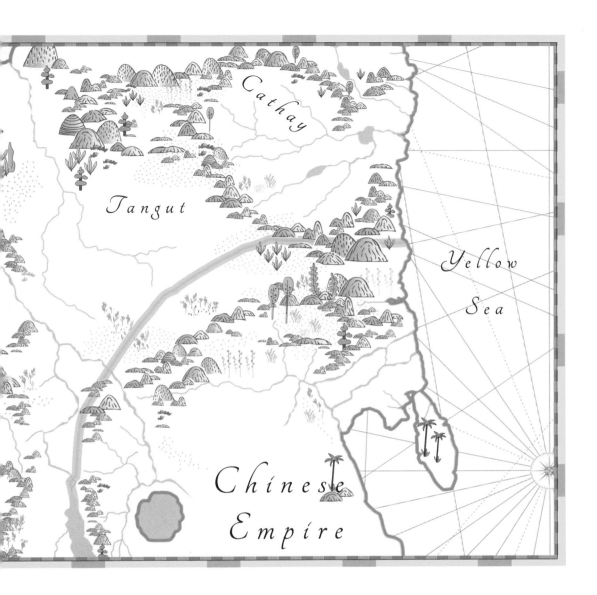

lo's travels. . . . On the map of Tartary in Joan Blaeu's *Atlas Maior*, which was compiled at the very beginning of the eighteenth century, dragons and devils are depicted in the Lop Desert, west of the Great Wall of China: as if to recall the mythical and wonderful past of this fabulous land.

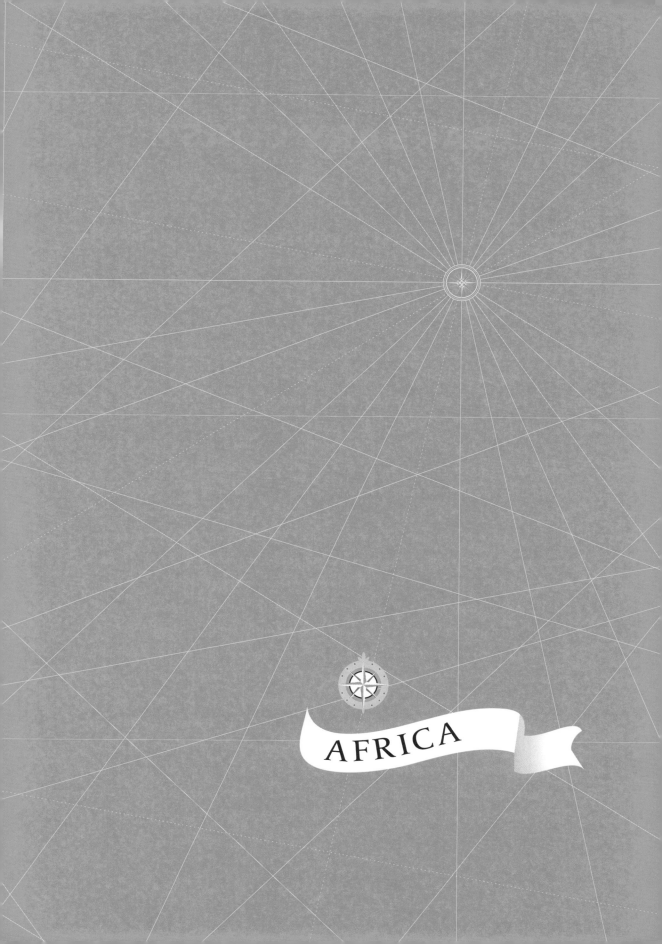

AFRICA

BARBARY COAST

At the Gates of Africa

IN 1415, the troops of Henry, King of Portugal, seized Ceuta. Names such as Guinea, Senegal, and Timbuktu made the young ruler, passionate about maps and the patron of sailors, dream. He, who would hardly ever leave the Algarve coast, or even his fort in Sagres, would earn himself the nickname "the Navigator."

Henry was a visionary who sensed that the city he had just captured was only the threshold to a gigantic land, a world, a continent bigger than any cosmographer expected. Following their sovereign's formidable intuition and unshakable faith, the Portuguese left the Barbary Coast behind and set off to conquer Africa, traveling along its western shores. So the Barbary Coast remained largely unknown.

Olfert Dapper, in his *Description of Africa*, would later explain that the country's name derived from *ber*, for "desert," "because this land was scarcely populated before the Arabs settled here: the inhabitants still bear the name Berbers." He continues: "Others argue its name to be of Latin origin, and that the Romans, who had conquered this province, called it Barbary in response to the fierce and barbaric mood of its inhabitants." As Montaigne would write later, "Each man labels as 'barbarism' anything he is not accustomed to" (translated by Jonathan Bennett). Leo Africanus, a Muslim converted to Christianity by Pope Leo X, was a traveler and geographer born in Granada, who composed a book in Arabic before self-translating it into Italian and Latin, which would long be considered the Vulgate on Africa. His description of the Barbary Coast was considered to be precise. However, Leo Africanus did not travel all over Africa; he only partly crossed the continent, from Morocco to Egypt, and up until the Niger River valley. A tremendously intelligent man, he was charged with many diplomatic missions and met and had exchanges with numerous merchants and dignitaries. And he read a lot. Latin texts, of course, but also those written by Arab chroniclers and geographers, including the great Muhammad al-Idrisi, unknown in the West at the time.

Extending from the Atlas Mountains to the Atlantic, the Mediterranean Sea, and the deserts of Libya and Egypt, "Barbaria" was one of the four divisions of Africa proposed by Leo

Africanus, along with Numidia, Libya, and the "Land of Negroes." Geographers after him would propose other divisions.

"This is the most noble and worthie region of all Africa, the inhabitants whereof are of a brown or tawnie colour, being a ciuill people, and prescribe wholsome lawes and constitutions vnto themselues" (translated by John Pory). It consists of four kingdoms: "Maroco" and Fez, each subdivided into seven provinces; "Tremizen" (Tlemcen), subdivided into three provinces; and Tunis, subdivided into four provinces. In these kingdoms and forests, there were apparently plenty of wild beasts, as well as monkeys, wild goats, lions, tigers, venomous snakes, birds of all kinds, and so on. According to Leo Africanus, the inhabitants of Barbary Coast are split across cities, where "the citizens applied themselues vnto some manuall art, or to husbandrie," and the countryside in the hinterland, where the "gouernours of the countrie attended their droues and flockes." The coastal region, with its "spatious plaine & many little hillocks," is very conducive to cultivation, as opposed to the Atlas Mountains, which are "exceeding colde and barren and bring foorth but small store of corne."

The kingdom of Morocco is "abounding with many droues and flockes of cattell: it is greene euery where, and most fertile of all things, which ferue for foode, or which delight the senses of smelling or feeing. It is altogither a plaine countrey, not much ynlike to Lombardie." This is the richest and most abundant part of Africa; in neighboring Libya, with its arid land unfit to be cultivated and brushed over by fierce sandstorms, the traveler already complains about thirst and the heat.

The inhabitants there fall into three categories: native Africans local to the place, Turks come here to make a fortune, and the Arabs of the deserts. Among Africans, there are whites, who live along the coasts and in the cities, corsairs, and Black people of the south. Enchantments and magic spells are part of their malicious customs, drawing on witches' incantations from the Alcoran, superstitions pronounced by soothsayers, and plain marabouts.

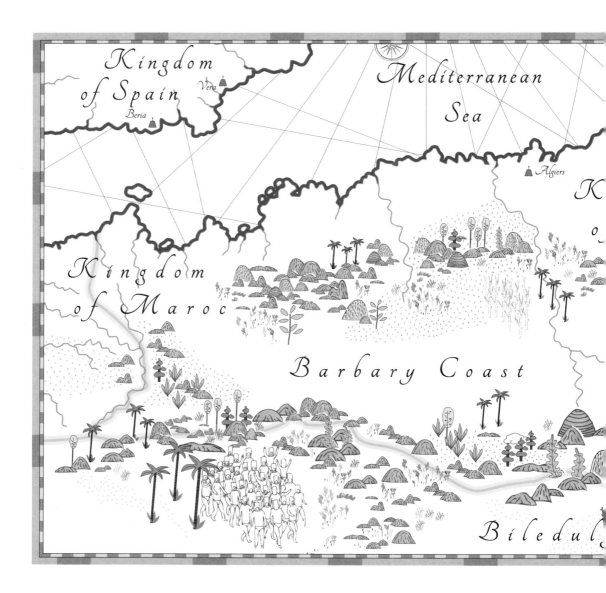

Leo Africanus notes that the Barbary Coast is thriving, that its kings and lords are immensely rich, and that besides their income, the number and splendor of their mosques are symbols of their affluence. He recounts that the Barbarian merchants are active, and that they trade on the banks of the Niger River, in the large cities up to the largest of them all: Timbuktu, where they go to sell woolen cloth transported from northern Europe, but also cattle hides, linen and cotton sheets, grapes, dates, figs, and so on. At the beginning of the sixteenth century, evoking opulent lands from which the riches came that one would find

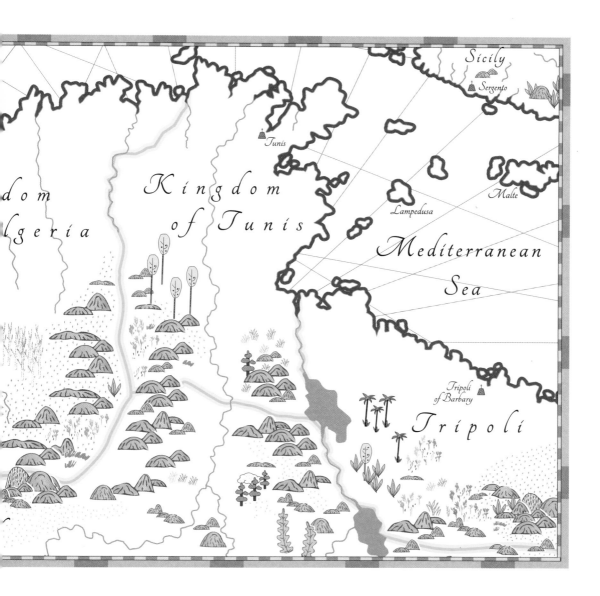

in Antwerp, an anonymous observer compares the Barbary Coast with Asia, Africa, and America: "If I take into account the singularities that America, Peru, and the entire New World sent there, and the riches that India, Guinea, the Barbary Coast, Asia, Africa, and Europe dispatch, I call Antwerp the mistress of all cities." The Barbary Coast of Leo Africanus, which takes up half of his monumental description, thus appeared in the fifteenth and sixteenth centuries as a rich, happy, and prosperous kingdom on a continent of which Europeans knew very little.

CAP BOJADOR

The Cape of Fear

LONG CONSIDERED TO BE the southern edge of the known world, Cape Bojador remained for Portuguese navigators the "Cape of Fear" for a long time. Remember the way the world was split in the minds of the ancient Greeks: they divided the world into five zones. Geographers called the region between the two temperate zones the "torrid zone," or perusta, meaning "burnt." In their encyclopedias, following in the vein of an ancient tradition that did not besmirch the Christian worldview, Vincent of Beauvais, Johannes de Sacrobosco, and Brunetto Latini note that the sun's rays burn so fiercely onto this part of the world as to make it uninhabitable. A European who had the misfortune of finding himself there would immediately turn black.

As the boundary between the temperate zone and the torrid zone, Cape Bojador is thus described in the chronicles: "It is clear that beyond this cape, no men or populations of any kind may exist. The land there is no less sandy than that of the deserts of Libya, where there is no water, no tree, no green grass."

Marco Polo claimed to have crisscrossed several lands of the area and emerged unscathed, but the fabulous interpretations prevailed in the imagination of the ancient Greeks, and the famous torrid zone remained an unsavory place to visit while acting as a foil and fantasy for Europeans.

The first attempts to cross the cursed cape were unsuccessful, and their outcome was bleak. Around 1346, the Catalan Jaime Ferrer disappeared off the coast of the Río de Oro. Some travelers, however, wanted to push further, such as the Frenchman Gadifer de la Salle, who wanted to "get news of Prester John and to get close to these territories whence so many goods and wealth come." In "the heroic tradition of the champions of the faith, the Saracen slayers, and anxious to lend Prester John a hand," in the well-chosen words of the historian Michel Mollat du Jourdin, the Lusitanian ruler Henry gave his financial support for companies tempted by the adventure. Adventurers of all stripes and colors were attracted by the lure of gold, the hunt for slaves, the trade in spices mixed with a vague adventurous spirit, and the desire to go on a crusade for the "true faith." Giving in to the siren song, the Venetian Alvise Cadamosto and the Genoese Antonietto Usodimare, seeking their fortune, left the Italian peninsula for Portugal, from where they sailed for the African coast. But, like their predecessors, they did not risk crossing the fateful cape.

Yet, King Henry could not get the idea out of his head. For a long time, Portuguese navigators paid no heed to their ruler's desires. Gomes Eanes de Zurara, a columnist for the kingdom and curator of the Royal Library at the Palace of the Alcáçova, evokes the reasons why "there was not one who dared to pass that Cape of Bojador" (translated by Charles Raymond Beazley and Edgar Prestage).

In his *Chronicle of the Discovery and Conquest of Guinea*, which traces the movements of the Portuguese from the capture of Ceuta in 1415 until the crossing of the mythical Cape Bojador by the navigator Gil Eanes in 1434, he successively evokes the ocean as a symbol of the unknown, of ships in distress, of being devoured, of bodies and souls being swallowed up. Determined not to lose body and soul in the water, sailors refused the leap into the unknown. They inherited this commendable prudence from their illustrious predecessors.

The same Gomes Eanes of Zurara provides us with the denouement of the tale: having captured Ceuta, the Portuguese were set to take on Africa by sailing along its shores. Galvanized by their visionary ruler Henry the Navigator, they would, for the first time, sail beyond the famous cape, triumphing over the sea, and their own fear.

A certain Gil Eanes managed the feat. It caused quite a stir. Contrary to the writings of the ancient Greeks, the adventurers encountered neither infernal whirlwinds nor magnetic mountains. Quite to the contrary: they discovered lands with abundant vegetation, and people who were nothing less than humans. In 1455, Pope Nicholas V "gives, concedes, and attributes in perpetuity" possession of all the lands south of Cape Bojador, all the way to Guinea, to the King of Portugal.

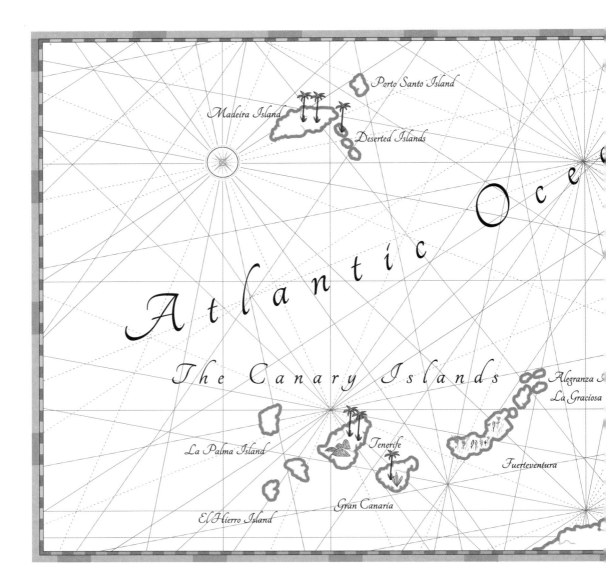

In 1460, the Portuguese navigator Diogo Gomes, recalling the fear Cape Bojador and the torrid zone triggered in people, wrote, "The very illustrious Ptolemy probably passed on to us many good lessons in geography, but he was wrong on this point. Thus, where he assumed an equinoctial region uninhabited due to an excess of heat, the Portuguese navigators have

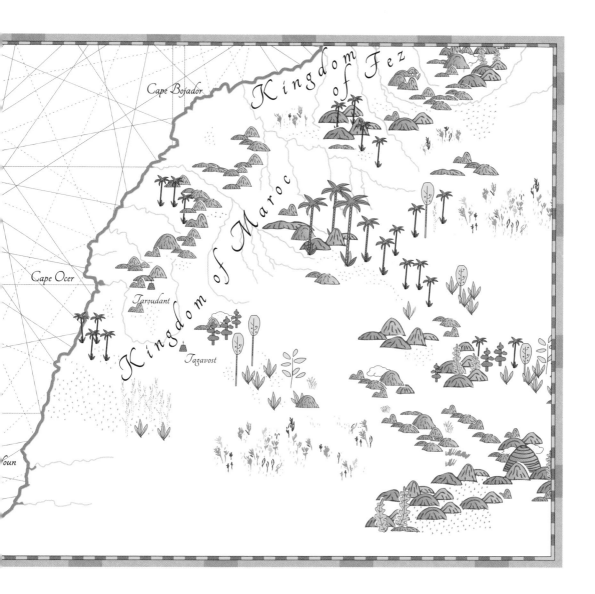

found an extremely populated region, rich in trees and plant life." Once they had gone beyond Cape Bojador, the Portuguese did not stop there. They would pass Cabo Blanco, Cap-Vert, Cape Palmas, Cape Three Points . . . and eventually circumnavigate Africa, opening a new passage to India, thus bidding farewell to their century-long fears.

CONGO

The Land of Cockaigne

"**KING DOM JOÃO II,** wishing to discover the East Indies, sent several ships along the coast of Africa, which, having found the Cape Verde Islands and the Island of St. Thomas, and running all along that coast, reached the River Zaire. . . . Later, . . . finding the merchandise open and profitable and the people amicable, several Portuguese remained there to learn the language, and to trade." (translated by Margarite Hutchinson). It is in this epic narrative that the Portuguese explorer Duarte Lopes recounts the arrival of his compatriots in the Congo in 1480.

In 1482, Diogo Cão erected a padrão on the north shore of the Zaire River to seal the possession of the lands in the name of the King of Portugal. The Zaire River divided the country into two kingdoms: Loango in the north, and the Congo in the south. The Portuguese presence bore expected spiritual fruits: the king of the Congo would convert to Christianity in 1491.

The Lusitanian peregrinations to the Congo, Guinea, and São Tomé would be recorded in several important volumes: João de Barros devoted the first volume of his *Décadas: La Relatione del Reame di Congo de Filippo Pigafetta* to them, compiled from notes taken by the Portuguese traveler Duarte Lopes. It originally appeared in Italian in Rome in 1591, then in Latin in the collected journeys published by the De Bry brothers in 1598 and 1624. The general map of Africa in these volumes depicts the Nile flowing into Lake Zaire, populated by strange "sea horses." The Mountains of the Moon of the southern Congo are adjoined by the so-called Ors Mountains. Travelers and readers of these books would be fascinated upon discovering these previously unknown lands. The fauna of the Congo makes you dream. Pufferfish with shield-shaped tails and hands, torpedoes or electric fish, and flying fish appear printed in a wondrous anthology. Almeida, following Father Bohvar's story, evokes a monstrous bird and wonders: Is this not the "red bird of the Arabs, one of those described in the novel about Sinbad?"

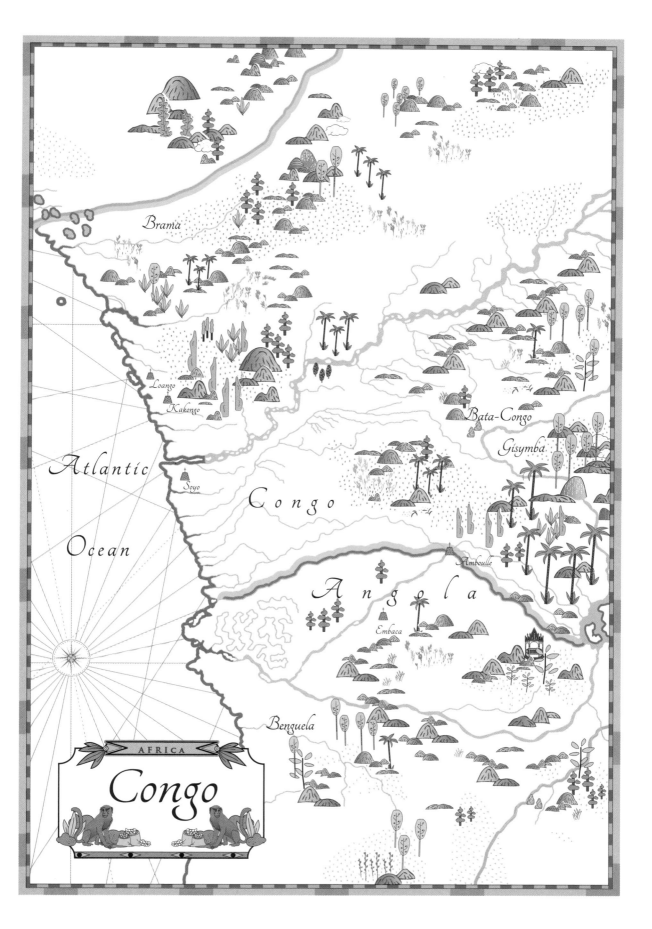

Brama

Loango

Kakongo

Atlantic

Soyo

Congo

Ocean

Bata-Congo

Gisymba

Amboulle

Angola

Embaca

Benguela

AFRICA

Congo

In the second chapter of the utopia *The Southern Land, Known by Gabriel de Foigny*, titled "Sadeur's Voyage to the Kingdom of Congo," the African kingdom appears as a genuine paradise on Earth, a place of abundance and all pleasures. Tradition has long situated the paradise on Earth in the east of a mythical Africa bordered by the Indus River. Herodotus recalled in his *Histories* the abundance that characterized tropical regions. Sadeur observes that the kingdom of Congo is half as populated as Portugal: reflecting on this stunning lack of people, he establishes a connection between the little energy the Indigenous people deploy to cultivate their land and their difficulty in ascertaining their offspring. This mythical Congo in *The Southern Land, Known*

is famous for the bounty of its soil, which "yields an abundance of produce without needing to be cultivated" (translated by David Fausett). "Everywhere the abundance of the land makes them vague, lazy, simple, and stupid." It ostensibly had the same effect on Sadeur and his companions!

Pufferfish with shield-shaped tails and hands, torpedoes or electric fish, and flying fish appear printed in a wondrous anthology.

After having stayed in Maninga for a few days, the capital of the kingdom, Sadeur receives his captain's permit to sail up the Zaire River "as far as the lake of that name." What he discovers there will astonish him to the point that he doubts anyone will believe his account. Who, in the West, might suspect that such a benevolent nature and such an impossible fauna could exist? The animals there are fabulous, fruit grows miraculously, and lush plants work wonders. Continuing his exploration of the area, Sadeur stops on the river Nile and then travels upstream to the source of the Cuama River—presumably the actual Zambezi River. He counts two / two hundred streams "rising in the mountains facing south,» called by the Spanish "Mountains of the Moon." Referring to the monsters that historians suspected in these places, Sadeur mentions a "neighboring people called Kaffirs by the Europeans or Tordi by the locals," savages who "cannot be humanized." Having reached the  end of their journey, Sadeur and his companions decide to return to Maninga by traveling downstream the Cariza River.

Encompassing a vast territory that exceeds the limits of present-day central Africa, the Congo of Foigny is a mythical place in terms of its dimensions, the beauty of its flora, and the singularity of its fauna. All travelers' tales and descriptions by cosmographers insist on the bounty of the Congolese natural world, which in its lushness provides for all the Indigenous people's needs. Some descriptions of the Congo sometimes recall those of the land of Cockaigne or Schlaraffenland, the country of the lazybones: a paradise where people do not have to work to live.

Later, the myth would change its face: from a kingdom of plenty, the Congo will turn into the heart of darkness and feed travelers' fantasies and fears, who will populate the land with ferocious animals and belligerent tribes hostile toward white people.

MEROË

BETWEEN THE THIRD CENTURY BCE and the fourth century CE, in the early days of Christianity, the kingdom of Meroë extended from the Blue Nile to the Atbarah River. In antiquity, in local, biblical, and Egyptian sources, Meroë is referred to as the "country of the Kush." Greek and Roman historians called the kingdom's territory, as well as all the lands that originated from it, Ethiopia or the "land of burned faces." For the ancient Greeks, for Diodorus of Sicily and Strabo in particular, this term encompassed what they called the "island of Meroë," that immense territory marked by three rivers: the Nile in the west, the Blue Nile in the southwest, and the Atbarah River in the northeast. In his *Histories*, Herodotus tells us that to reach Meroë from Elephantine, "a distance of twelve schoeni must be passed in the foregoing manner. After that, you come to a level plain, where there is an island in the Nile, called Takhompso. . . . Then you disembark and journey along the riverbank for forty days; for there are sharp projecting rocks in the Nile and many reefs, through which no boat can pass. . . . You take boat again and so travel for twelve days until you come to a great city called Meroe, which is said to be the capital of all Ethiopia."

But to trace the origins of this amazing civilization, we must return to the third millennium BCE. Opposite the powerful Egyptian Empire, the kingdom of Kerma was in the making, which, despite its modest size, soon began to flourish. Proud Egypt could not allow this kingdom to prosper with such impunity. Making conquests, it eventually subjugated and annexed the kingdom. In the eighth century BCE, however, an independent power founded a new kingdom, farther south: Napata. But, like Kerma, Napata was unable to defy its powerful neighbors for very long. The Assyrians invaded it, forcing its people to submit or leave. Opting for departure, the survivors of Napata would form another kingdom, even farther south: Meroë. For seven centuries, it would be one of the most illustrious civilizations of antiquity. Strongly influenced by its powerful neighbors,

Between the Blue Nile and the Atbarah River, the kingdom of Meroë was, for seven centuries, one of the most illustrious civilizations of antiquity.

the Egypt of the Ptolemies, the Greece of Alexander the Great, Persia, and the Roman Empire, it built many necropolises and pyramids, reaching its peak at the beginning of the first century BCE. The kingdom of Meroë was renowned for the splendor of its culture and the wisdom of its queens, which became known as the "Kandakes." The kingdom thus aroused the desire of the Romans. In 33 BCE, the Kandake Amanishakheto refused to submit and sent her troops to challenge the Roman legions in the north of the country. Rejected and humiliated, the Romans gave up on conquering Meroë. The kingdom would last for a few more centuries before, like many civilizations, it would disappear under mysterious circumstances.

But the story does not end there. At the beginning of the nineteenth century, Frédéric Cailliaud, an explorer turned official mineralogist to the Wāli of Egypt, Muhammad Ali, traveled back up the Nile valley. He would become one of the first Europeans to enter Ethiopia. In April 1821, he finally saw the ruins of Meroë. "Imagine the joy I experienced upon discovering the peaks of a multitude of pyramids whose tips were illuminated in gold by the rays of a sun still low on the horizon!" he writes. Meroë, which until then had appeared only in the Bible and texts from antiquity and had thus been taken for a legendary kingdom, was no longer a fable. Back in France, he noted down his extraordinary discovery in *Voyage à Méroé (Journey to Meroë)*.

Cailliaud had settled in Nantes to perform the duties of assistant curator at the Museum of Natural History. He probably believed that he had discovered the key wonders of Meroë. He did not yet know that a certain Giuseppe Ferlini would make the most fabulous find of them all. The Italian adventurer and military doctor in the pay of Muhammad Ali of

Egypt would visit the site of the capital of the ancient kingdom of Meroë, hoping to find a treasure. After all, Heinrich Schliemann had found the treasure of King Priam! So why not him? Following the plans and drawings made by Cailliaud, whose book the adventurer was carrying with him, Ferlini dismantled several pyramids stone by stone. Without success. But his tenacity paid off. Not afraid to handle explosive finds, he put his hand on a fabulous treasure: that of Kandake Amanishakheto, the most famous of all the Kandakes of Meroë! Amanishakheto the rebellious, Amanishakheto the proud! The woman who had tamed the Roman legions and allowed her people to live in peace for several centuries! Ferlini sold the treasure to the museums of Munich and Berlin, having left behind—unscrupulously pursuing his dream—a true field of ruins.

Meroë would continue to fascinate and attract looters and adventurers, but also archeologists, who would eventually save it. And to this date, the mythical city has not revealed all its secrets, since its script has not yet been fully deciphered.

MUTAPA

Kingdom of Gold and Diamonds

ON OLD MAPS, "Monomotapa" is written in large capitals across all of southern Africa. Cartographers employed this name, based on travelers' reports, to fill a huge gap at the bottom of the map of the Black Continent.

Of all continents, Africa remained the least known for the longest time, with travelers having explored only its coasts. To remedy these enormous shortcomings, cartographers first filled in these lands with monsters, and then by evoking a fabulous kingdom: Mutapa.

When the Portuguese circumnavigated Africa to reach India, they punctuated the route with trading posts. That is how places such as Sofala, Quelimane, Mozambique, Mombasa, and Malindi were born. Having found out from the local population about the existence of gold mines in a fabulous remote kingdom, the settlers planned to discover it and would obstinately pursue this search for years. This land, Ophir, would eventually lead to the discovery—or invention—of Mutapa. In 1508, in his *Esmeraldo of Orbis Situ*, Duarte Pacheco wrote: "Your captains discovered anew the great mine which some hold to be that of Ophir and is now called Çofala" (translated by George H. T. Kimble). But the gold there was not as abundant as they had hoped. The mythical kingdom of Ophir must therefore lie elsewhere. So they left. In 1514, Captain Antonio Fernandes, after leaving Sofala, explored the interior and followed the Zambezi River, convinced that this river was a sure route to the heart of the Black Continent, and thus to discover the kingdom of Ophir. Several trading posts were founded along the river. Half a century later, missionaries arrived at a land similar to Ophir in many ways.

The kingdom of Ophia was founded by King Nyatsimba, whose title Mwene Mutapa refers to his duties as a military and religious leader. The term "Mwene Mutapa," originally used to designate the sovereign, was distorted by travelers and then quickly used to refer to the

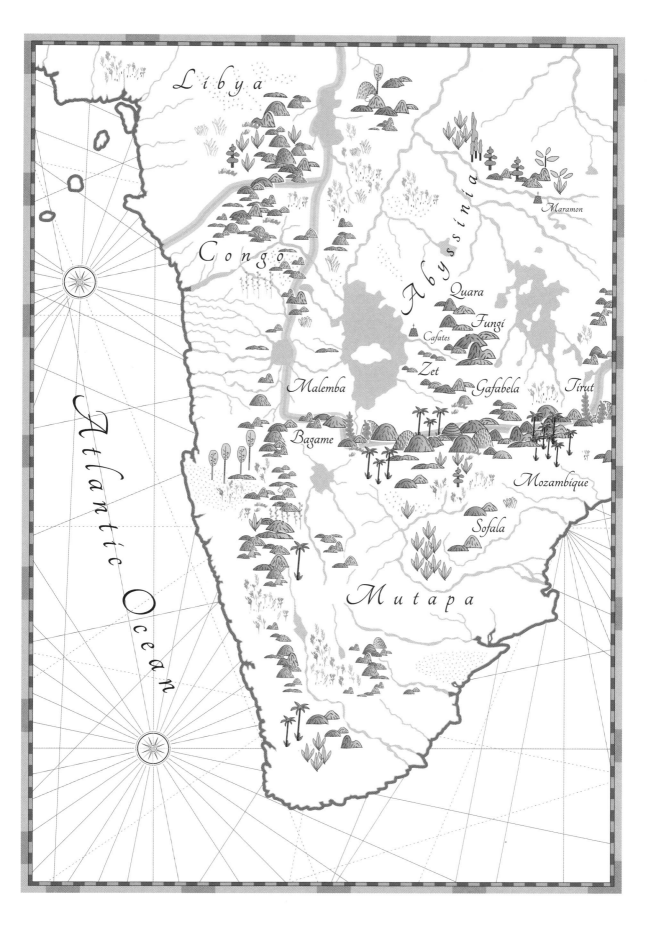

Libya

Congo

Abyssinia

Maramon

Quara

Fungi

Cafates

Zet

Gafabela

Tirut

Malemba

Bagame

Mozambique

Atlantic Ocean

Sofala

Mutapa

kingdom itself. Merchants, missionaries, and chroniclers would use it in several stories, letters, and even royal and religious correspondence. In 1660, the Portuguese missionaries met Matopo, the son of Nyatsimba and heir to a kingdom in which they had discovered amber, gum, ivory, and gold. However, Mutapa would not become a new Peru, to the great displeasure of the young Portuguese sovereign Sebastian! Moreover, the subjects of the Mutapa kingdom did not let themselves be stripped of their assets so easily, and they fiercely fought back. But the Portuguese did not give up on their dreams of gold, and continued to dispatch expeditions to locate the mines containing the precious yellow metal. They explored the neighboring lands of Mutapa—though the last word on the kingdom had not yet been uttered.

In Portugal, the historian João de Barros was one of the first to make mention of Monomotapa, in the tenth book of his *Décadas*. It had not yet received its final name, so Barros calls it "Benomotapa." He praised its political system, his polygamous sovereign, and the respect he commanded. The Jesuit Luis Frois, on the basis of a letter addressed to him by a friend of the sovereign, described in lush detail the protocol in use at the court of Mutapa, which usually characterized the pomp at great courts. In these accounts, it had become equal to the greatest courts in Europe. But Filippo Pigafetta's and João dos Santos's witness accounts would eventually make Mutapa one of the most fascinating regions of the Black Continent. Filippo Pigafetta was a papal chamberlain who wrote, in Italian, on the basis of notes by Portuguese traveler Duarte Lopes, the *Relatione del Reame di Congo*, published in Rome in 1591. He writes: "From the shoars and Coast, that lyeth betweene the two foresaide riuers of Magnice and Cuama, within the land spreadeth the Empire of Monomotapa, where there is verye great store of Mines of Golde, which is carryed from thence into all the regions thereaboutes, and into Sofala, and into the other parts of Africa. And some there be that wil say that Salomons Golde, which he had for the Temple of Ierusalem, was brought by sea out of these Countreyes. . . . For in the Countries of Monomotapa, there doe remain to this day many ancient buildings of great worke and singular Architecture . . . the like whereof are not be seene in all the Prouinces adioyning. The Empire of Monomotapa is very great, and for people infinite. They are Gentiles and Pagans, of colour blacke, very couragious in warre . . . and swift of foote. Ther are many Kinges,

> Golde is carryed from thence into all the regions thereaboutes, and into Sofala, and into the other parts of Africa. And some there be that wil say, that Salomons Golde, which he had for the Temple of Ierusalem, was brought by sea out of these Countreyes.

that are vassalles and subiectes of Monomotapa. . . . It bordereth towards the South ypon the Lordes of the Cape of Good-Hope" (translated by Abraham Hartwell). A Dominican missionary dispatched to India, João dos Santos took the road via southern Africa, where he would stay from 1586 to 1597. Back in Portugal in 1600, he began work on his masterpiece, a volume combining his experience and his readings. Although the book is titled *Ethiopia Oriental*, it is really dedicated to Mutapa. João dos Santos wanted to be exhaustive. He addresses a jumble of topics, from topography, population, and manners to religious practices, wildlife, flora, and various riches. After him, cosmographers would go even further. They would become unstoppable in terms of depicting the splendor of the court and the profusion of gold mines. So much so that in the sixteenth and seventeenth centuries, Mutapa would inherit all the characteristics of Prester John's kingdom at the end of the Middle Ages.

THE LAND OF THE MANGBETU

In the Heart of Darkness

THE CONGO, Mutapa, the kingdom of Saba', and the land of Good Hope are not the only countries to excite the imagination of Western travelers. The land of the Mangbetu also had its hour of glory at the end of the nineteenth century, at the height of the colonial era. The Mangbetu, whose founder was King Nabiembali, allegedly came from Nubia. Following alliances with the Mbuti, they then settled in the present-day Congo in the seventeenth century. It was under the leadership of their sovereign Mounza that, in the nineteenth century, they had driven out the Arabs and had entered into conflict with their neighbors, the Niam-Niam people (now Zande)—they were famously said to have tails.

In the mid-nineteenth century, the traveler and naturalist Georg Schweinfurth met them and lived among them. Funded by the Humboldt Foundation, he explored the Congo-Nile watershed and entered the court of Mounza, king of the Mangbetu. The dreaded monarch had become famous for driving the Arabs and the Zande out of his country. Like the Zulu strategist Chaka, Mounza subordinated his enemies and subjects to the same terror and cruelty. His palace, built in the trees in the middle of a dense forest, would fascinate Schweinfurth, whose story, *Im Herzen von Afrika* (*The Heart of Africa*), went on to captivate many readers. When Schweinfurth entered the Mangbetu kingdom, accompanying the Arab leader Abd-es-Samate, he was, like his peers, in search of the mythical source of the Nile. For him, the country of the Mangbetu constituted only a

> For them, human flesh was a usual meal, alongside elephant, dog, and game birds.

pit stop. But the symbolic privilege of being the first white person to be introduced to the court of King Mounza did not bear the expected fruit: the tyrannical sovereign, determined to retain his commercial monopoly on trading copper with Nubia, did not allow his host to continue on his route south. This stop would allow the young explor-

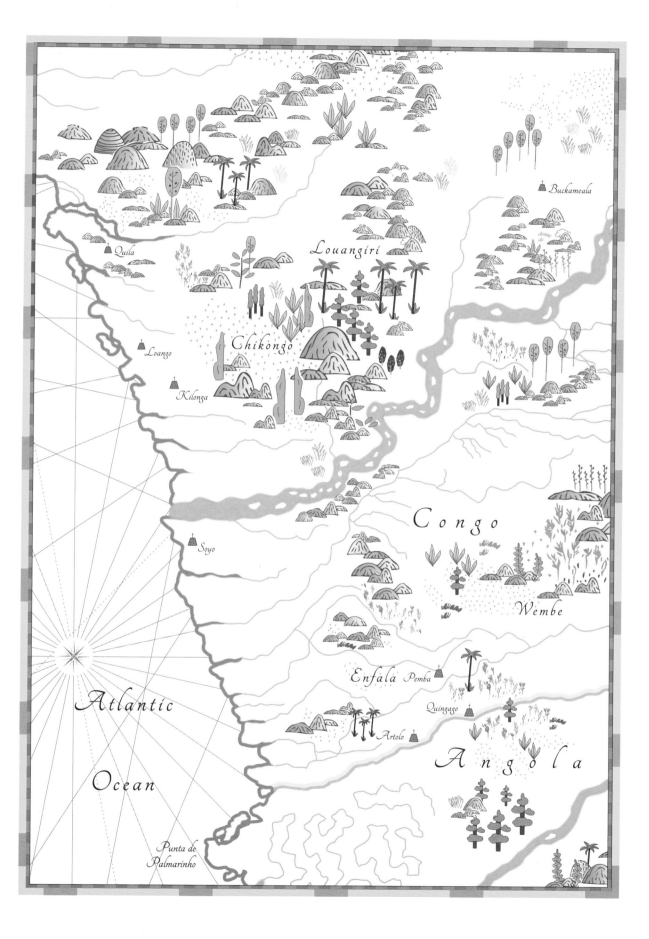

Quila

Louangiri

Buckameala

Loango

Chikongo

Kilonga

Congo

Soyo

Wembe

Enfala Pemba

Quingago

Atlantic

Artolo

Angola

Ocean

Punta de
Palmarinho

er to learn about the local customs, which were very different from Western habits: the Mangbetu were cannibals. Schweinfurth's descriptions of their orgies, in which only men participated, show meticulous detail. For them, human flesh was a usual meal, alongside elephant, dog, and game birds. Their enemies' territories were also hunting grounds for them: "The carcasses of all who fall in battle are distributed upon the battle-field and are prepared by drying for transport to the homes of the conquerors" (translated by Ellen E. Frewer). Prisoners and children, considered sweets and destined for the king, were reserved for later. However, the practices of the Mangbetu did not immeasurably disturb Schweinfurth. And it is with no apparent upset that he describes a group of women who "were engaged in the task of scalding the hair off the lower half of a human body. The operation, as far as it was effected, had changed the black skin into a fawny grey, and the disgusting sight could not fail to make me think of the soddening and scouring of our fatted swine. On another occasion I was in a hut and observed a human arm hanging over the fire, obviously with the design of being at once dried and smoked."

These orgies allowed Schweinfurth to build an extraordinary collection of skulls, which he would leave to the Berlin Museum. After three weeks among the Mangbetu, Schweinfurth began his return journey, forced to stop his quest for the source of the Nile. The kingdom and court of the Mangbetu, as the German explorer saw and described them, would not survive much longer. In 1873, the tyrannical Mounza was overthrown and murdered, his palace set alight, and his kingdom divvied up. But his reign

Prisoners and children, considered sweets and destined for the king, were reserved for later.

and the magnificence of his court would become immortalized, thanks to Schweinfurth's irreplaceable account but also to his epigones—including a certain Jules Verne. In what is probably one of his lesser-known Extraordinary Voyages series texts, *A Singular Forest*, the novelist tells of the life of a forest people, the Wagddis.

Dancing to the music of the Freischütz by Schubert, this avatar of the Mangbetu would become the famous missing link sought by naturalists of the eighteenth and nineteenth centuries. Following the lead of Jules Verne, and with much literary reinforcement, generations of anthropologists would go to Africa in search of the descendants of the Mangbetu and the Zande people, in the hope of meeting the last cannibals of central Africa. In vain. While this practice may have been common in King Mounza's time, it is mostly a myth and part of the image of the evil "savage" that Western colonizers cherished.

PRESTER JOHN'S KINGDOM

The Mysterious Christian Land

IN 1441, at the Council of Florence, representatives of a mysterious Christian kingdom located in the East of the African continent were introduced. The Council Fathers were in the middle of a debate on the schism-shaking Christians in the East and the West. As if the heated debates were not enough, these men from a land believed to have been taken over by heathens brought news of the existence of believers in Christ at the heart of the land of Cham! This information, if true, would be incredible!

In 1447, a Genoese merchant of noble extraction, Antonio Malfante, arrived in Honaine. From there, he went to Sijilmasa, a city in the Sahara Desert, before following in the footsteps of the Arab traveler Ibn Battuta to Tuat. He arrived in Tamentit and sent his superior Giovanni Mariono a report on his exploration of the region. He mixed up the Niger River and the Nile—a common mistake at the time. In his letter, he wrote: "From what I can understand, these people neighbour on India. Indian merchants come hither, and converse through interpreters. These Indians are Christians, adorers of the cross" (translated by G. R. Crone). For Giovanni Mariono, there is no longer any doubt: there is a mysterious Christian kingdom in these parts. In 1450, in Naples, Pietro Rambulo presented himself to the Dominican Pietro Ranzano as the ambassador of a certain Prester John, as envoy to the King of Aragon. His story is, to say the least, incredible: he had been at the court of Prester John for a long time and allegedly married an Ethiopian woman with whom he has seven children, all of whom raised "in a Latin way and in the Catholic religion." It was Prester John himself who, after having charged him with missions to Cathay, India, and Ceylon, has sent him to the sovereign of Aragon.

Pietro Ranzano was astounded by the description that Rambulo gave him of the kingdom of the amazing Prester John. His empire was said to be in Abyssinia. He apparently ruled over twelve kingdoms governed by princes, priests, and merchants.

The language spoken in this thoroughly hierarchical state was Chaldean. Its inhabitants, all baptized Christians, are said to be marked with a red iron. And, to top off this already stupefying testimony, Rambulo claimed that Prester John was a direct descendant of the Queen of Saba', and that he commanded an army of several hundred riders and six thousand elephants. A far-greater army than that of Hannibal! Rambulo gifted a map to the Dominican outlining the best route to reach the fabulous Christian kingdom from the city of Alexandria in Egypt . . .

These men from a land believed to have been taken over by heathens brought news of the existence of believers in Christ at the heart of the land of Cham!

Resolved to discovering this gigantic and legendary Christian kingdom in Africa, the Portuguese sovereign John II dispatched an expedition. What did it matter that Ethiopia was far from the trade route to India: John II seized the opportunity and charged one of his captains, Pero da Covilhan, with finding a route to reach the Indian Ocean through the Red Sea.

From Aden, Covilhan reached Calicut, then Ormus, and finally Sofala. Arrived at the fabulous court of the mythical Prester John, he would remain with his host until his death after 1520. The enterprise bore fruit: relations were finally established between Prester John and Manuel the Fortunate, who succeeded John II on the Portuguese throne. In the meantime, one part of the mystery of the enigmatic Prester John was resolved: he was none other than the Negus, the Monophysite Christian emperor of Abyssinia. In 1520, the ambassador Rodrigo de Lima, accompanied by the Dominican Francisco Alvares, embarked on a journey to Prester John's court and invested with an impressive number of missions, including the reconnaissance of a new commercial route, the integration of the church of the African Christian kingdom into the fold of the Roman Church, and the negotiation of an alliance against the Turks. What a schedule!

In 1540, Francisco Alvares, returning to Portugal, published a veritable tome about Prester John's kingdom: *Ho Preste Joan das Indias*. On the basis of material gathered by Pero da Covilhan and on his own observations, Alvares provides a rich and precise description of the Negus's kingdom. Although criticized by João de Barros, his account, reprinted and extensively translated, would remain the only serious document on Prester John's kingdom for a long time. But it would be Filippo Pigafetta's *Relatione del Reame di Congo*, partly inspired by João de Barros's volume, that would receive the most remarkable fortune and would put the kingdom of Prester John on the mythical map for travelers, by providing a fabulous description: "And now forasmuch as we are to speake of the Empire of Prete Gianni, who is the greattest and the richest Prince in all Africa. . . . The Confines of his estate are these, viz. towards the North-East, and the East, the greater parte of the Red Sea: towards the North, Aegypt: towardes the West, the Desertes of Nubia, and towards the South the countrey of Mohene-mugi: & so in a grosse and generall account, the Empire of this Christian King may happely bee in compasse some foure thousand miles. . . . His people are of diuers colours, as white, blacke, and a middle colour betweene both: they are of a very good stature, and haue good countenances. . . . These people are in a manner Christians. For they doo obserue certaine ceremonies of the Lawe of the Hebrewes. . . . The principall Cittie, where he most remayneth and keepeth his Court, is called Bel-Malechi. He ruleth ouer many Prouinces that haue their seuerall Kinges. His estate is very rich, and aboundeth in Golde, in Siluer, in precious stones" (translated by Abraham Hartwell). The myth of Prester John's kingdom will haunt the spirits until the end of the sixteenth century.

THE KINGDOM OF SABA'

The Queen's Gold

THE MYTH OF THE KINGDOM OF SABA' is in many ways connected with that of Prester John, and, of course, with that of King Solomon's gold mines.

Around 1400, the young Sicilian Pietro Rambulo left Messina to explore the world, beginning—since you ought to start somewhere—with the Italian peninsula, the south of France, and Spain. Upon his arrival in Venice, he sailed for the Barbary Coast and traveled across the north of the African continent for thirty years. Around 1430, in Cairo, he met an ambassador of the Negus, the emperor of Ethiopia, the one in whom Christianity would want to see the ruler of an immense Christian kingdom in the land of Cham: Prester John. The ambassador invited him to the court of the Negus.

Pietro Rambulo, rich in experience and with excellent knowledge of many languages, immediately attracted the good grace of the Negus, who appointed him an ambassador and charged him with missions to Cathay, India, Taprobana, and then Aragon and Naples. There, in 1450, he met a Dominican, a Sicilian like himself, for whom he would paint a rich picture of the fabulous kingdom and the venerable monarch whose ambassador he had the honor of being. For the monk, there was no doubt that the kingdom described by his compatriot was the famous Christian kingdom in the land of Cham, which travelers had mentioned without ever having been able to accurately locate it. And he grew certain that its sovereign was the no-less-famed Prester John.

Pietro Rambulo also gave him information about another legendary figure: the Queen of Saba'. Speaking of his knowledge of the region, Rambulo maintained that the king of the earth "called Habbas by the Saracens, Habbassia by the Latins"—that is, Abyssinia—the Negus, was a direct descendant of the Queen of Saba'. Who is this queen? She is mentioned in many traditions. According to the Bible, she was a woman of extraordinary beauty who visited Solomon in Israel and gifted him perfumes, precious stones, and gold. Solomon is said to have opened up his palace, his court, and his kingdom to her. Won over, she returned to her kingdom, praising God for having placed a man of such great wisdom as Solomon on

84

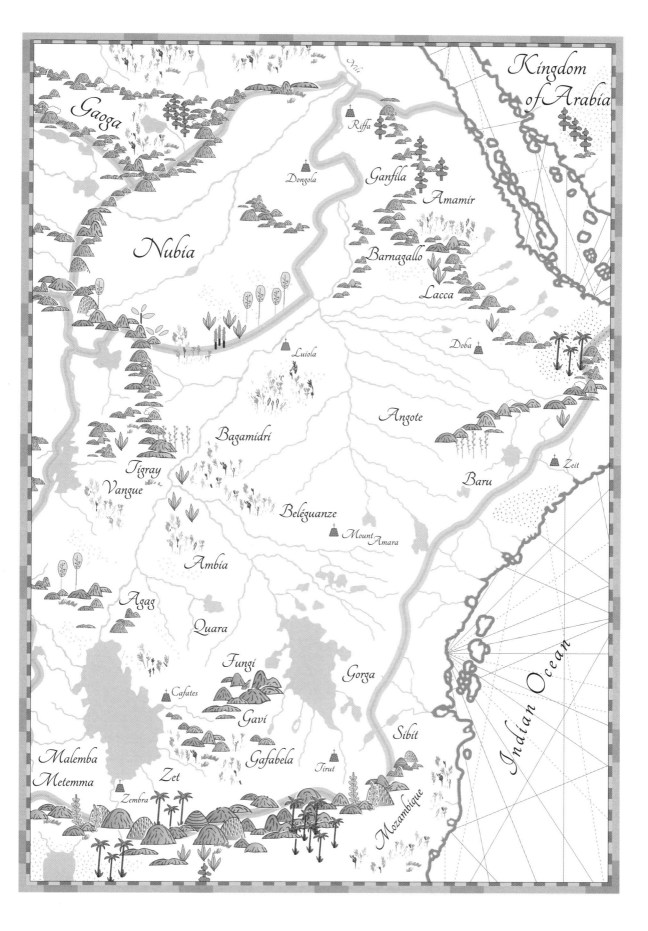

the throne of Israel. The Koran features a very similar version of the legend, adding that after her visit, the queen converted to "the faith of the one God."

In some traditions, the Queen of Saba' appears as Solomon's temptress, both witch and sorceress, a Black Circe or Calypso. This is how she is depicted on an altarpiece in Klosterneiburg Abbey dating from the end of the twelfth century. Until the fifteenth century, in the iconography of Rhineland Germany, the Queen of Saba' was sometimes Black with blond hair, sometimes Caucasian, a magician, temptress, or demonic spirit. Yet, all traditions agree that she owned immeasurable wealth. For decades, trusting more or less well-informed travelers, her kingdom would be the target of expeditions throughout the Black Continent and variably located in the south of the Barbary Coast, Numidia, Libya, or the Land of Negroes.

In the seventeenth century, when some mines and ruins of what was once the kingdom of Zimbabwe were discovered, explorers were yet again convinced that they had found Ophir, the kingdom of Saba'. Perfumes, gems, gold, ivory, slaves, monkeys, and peacocks are described in abundant detail in 1 Kings in the Bible. In his *Décadas*, João de Barros claimed that the discovered ruins were the remains of the storehouse in which the Queen of Saba' kept her wealth. And in his *Relatione del Reame di Congo*, Filippo Pigafetta, referring to Mutapa, assured readers that gold is extracted there in such quantities that the surplus is exported to neighboring countries and kingdoms.

Combining the myth of the Queen of Saba' with that of Solomon, people immediately inferred that this was where the gold had come from with which the king built his temple in Jerusalem.

The legends of King Solomon's gold mines and the kingdom of Saba' might have disappeared from popular imagination, had it not been for the nineteenth-century English novelist Henry Rider Haggard, who based his successful novel on the myth: *King Solomon's Mines*.

Haggard, taking advantage of the mystery surrounding an unknown African continent, tells the story of a group of explorers in search of a missing relative in Africa. During their search, they discover the famous mines of King Solomon. The novel and the cinematic adaptations based on this romantic story would fascinate generations of readers and spectators to come. Yet, this had less to do with the plot—common enough for its time—than with the author's ability to enchant an audience by connecting the ongoing dream of gold and diamonds hidden on an unexplored continent with the fabulous legend of a king and a queen from a bygone era.

For decades, trusting more or less well-informed travelers, this kingdom would be the target of expeditions throughout the Black Continent and variably located in the south of the Barbary Coast, Numidia, Libya, or the Land of Negroes.

THE SOURCE OF THE NILE

The Ways of Heaven

WE KNOW HOW ENCHANTING the river Nile is. A source of life in the middle of one of the world's most arid deserts, it has witnessed the most fascinating of civilizations flourish. And the source of this river, in which Moses was plunged and which Yahweh struck, are certainly among the mysteries that have long aroused the imagination of travelers, cosmographers, and cartographers. It does not surprise then that this river, steeped in history that seems to be linked to the history of God himself, is supposed to lead to paradise on Earth. Thus, locating the source of the Nile would become for generations of explorers and scholars the sesame enabling them to reach the biblical Eden.

While Martin Behaim's globe contains a fair number of errors, the German cosmographer merits not disguising places that were difficult to locate, such as Iceland, Saint Brendan, Cathay and Cipangu, Cape Verde, the Cape of Good Hope, or the Mountains of the Moon—and the source of the Nile, which it places somewhere in the vastness of Ethiopia.

In 1540, Francisco Alvares, a companion to the ambassador Rodrigo of Lima, published *Ho Preste Joam das Indias*, an account of his stay in Prester John's kingdom, which he locates close to the source of the river Nile without being able to pinpoint them precisely. Ten years later, Leo Africanus, in his "Africa," published in *Primo volume delle navagationi* by Giovanni Battista Ramusio, delivered a detailed description of Africa that he divided into four major parts: the Barbary Coast, Numidia, Libya, and the Land of Negroes. It is in the latter that he addresses the enigma of the source of the Nile. Leo Africanus explains that the Land of Negroes is crisscrossed in its entirety by the Niger River, which draws its source from a large lake situated east of the continent. It is in the same lake that the Nile has its source, before turning westward to tumble toward the Atlantic Ocean.

In the same era, other authors argued that "the Niger is a branch of the Nile that disappears underground and re-emerges in that place, forming this lake."

In 1578, Duarte Lopes explored the Congo and then Angola, probably intending to get back to the Zambezi River. Having pondered the origins of Africa's great rivers, he was trying

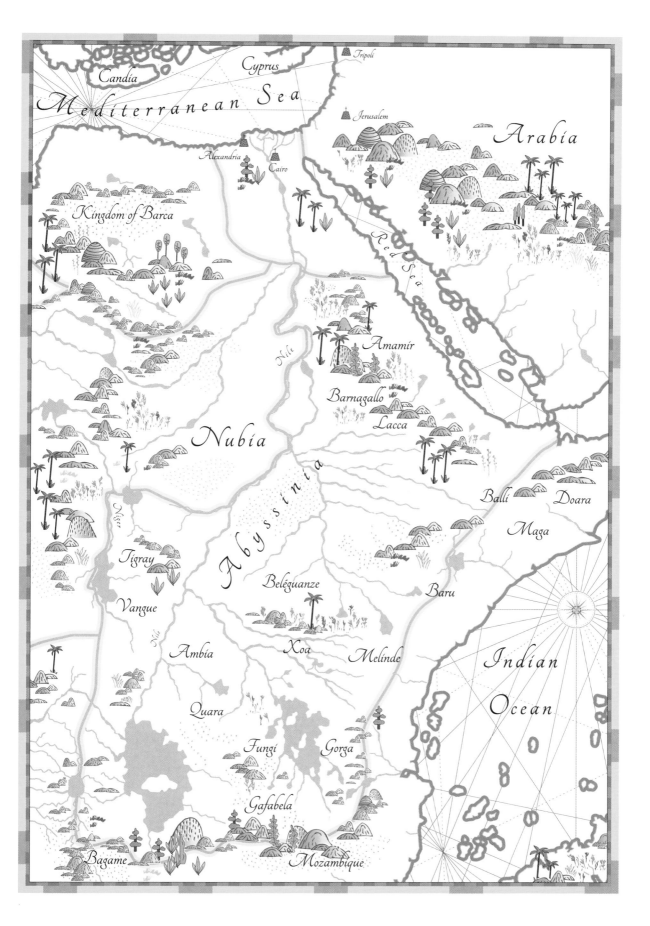

to gather information about the source of the Nile, which was the subject of much controversy. Like his contemporaries, Duarte Lopes harbored the conviction that all these rivers had sources, undoubtedly located in the region of these great lakes. He had no specific information about this and failed in his attempt to locate it.

In 1607, the Dominican missionary João dos Santos published his *Ethiopia Oriental*, which focused mainly on Mutapa. This man of God had lived in Sofala for ten years, from 1585 to 1595, so his account is pretty precise. Like his peers writing about the region, he tackles the unavoidable question of the source of the Nile. He gathered information and finally inferred that it must be in the vicinity of the sources of the Zambezi, the Congo, and the Gihon, the latter of which was considered at the time to be one of the four rivers of paradise.

In 1618, Father Páez published a *Historia de Etiopia*. When he put his account to paper, he did not yet know that he would be one of the first European travelers to reach and de-

A source of life in the middle of one of the world's most arid deserts, the Nile has witnessed the most fascinating of civilizations flourish. And the source of this river, in which Moses was plunged and which Yahweh struck, are certainly among the mysteries that have long aroused the imagination of travelers, cosmographers, and cartographers.

scribe Lake Tana as well as the source of the Blue Nile. In his *Introductionis in universam geographiam, tam veterem quam novam libri VI*, published after his death in 1626, the German geographer Philippe Clüver, or Cluverius, tries to trace the evolution of every part of the world since ancient times. He tackles the mystery of Atlantis, the Hyperboreans—and the famous source of the Nile. Without success.

To solve this difficult issue, geographers, cartographers, and cosmographers ended up depicting a single huge lake in the heart of Africa, or a mosaic of lakes, from which all the great rivers of the Black Continent flowed: the Zambezi, the Zaire, the Niger, and the Nile. Utopians were not satisfied with this. Gabriel de Foigny in his *The Southern Land, Known*, for example, attributed the same source to the Cuama River and the Nile by letting it spring from an enormous lake in the center of Africa. It would take until 1863 for the mystery of the Nile's source to finally be solved by the English team of John Speke, Samuel, and Florence Baker.

THE LANDS OF GOOD HOPE

IN THE FOURTEENTH CENTURY, the only parts of Africa known in Europe were the Barbary Coast, Libya, Ethiopia, and the regions around the Mediterranean discovered by the Romans. And while Arab merchants, taking over from Arab scholars, made Egypt and Abyssinia known, the torrid zone of the southern continent remained terra incognita. People would imagine regions dried out by the sun and simply uninhabitable. They would dream of fabulous animals and monstrous breeds: Blemmyes, monopods, monoculi, and baboons.

When Portuguese sailors, at the behest of their sovereign Henry the Navigator, who was passionate about cartography, explored the West Coast of the African continent, they outdid each other in terms of caution, fearing they would be swallowed up by waves of sea monsters, and trembling at the prospect of having their sails go up in flames. Cape after cape, however, they progressed, determined to open a new route to India. In 1434, Gil Eanes crossed Cape Bojador without a hitch, hitherto considered the point beyond which no one could venture without risking a safe return. This feat dispelled the fear of magic that still held back the Portuguese navigators. In 1488, Bartolomeu Dias de Novaes reached a cape dominated by a mountain with a flat top like a table. The wind blew in unbridled gusts. He called it "the cape of storms." Having reached the most southerly point of Africa, he began traveling up north along the continent's eastern coasts. But his crew, seized by the terror of the unknown in front of them, forced him to turn back when they reached the Río do Infante, and to return to Portugal.

However, his journey was not in vain. King John II, firmly convinced that India was very close, decided to give the "Cape of Storms" a name commensurate with his vision. He baptized it the "Cape of Good Hope." But it would be his successor, Manuel I, who entrusted Vasco da Gama with the mission of "circumnavigating" Africa to reach India. Spices and precious stones were not their only objects of desire. They also wanted to reach the mythical kingdom of Prester John to seal an alliance with him against the peo-

ple of the Fertile Crescent. In 1497, Vasco da Gama left the Tagus River at the head of four ships. He dropped anchor at the Cape of Good Hope to top off their supply of clean water, then continued on his way. He would carry out his mission and reach Calicut, India.

> While the colony and its immediate vicinity were well known, the hinterland remained the domain of the most persistent of dreams.

Unlike Portugal, the United Provinces not only saw the Land of Good Hope as a strategic pit stop but set to establish a colony there under the authority of Jan van Riebeeck, as early as 1652. Originally consisting of a fort and a garden, the colony maintained excellent relations with the Indigenous population, the Hottentots (now Khoekhoe), to the extent that it worried the Gentlemen Seventeen: the supervisory authority of the Dutch East India Company was offended by the growing number of mixed unions. The colony would become so prosperous that it would arouse the desire of other large European nations. Ships making their way to India would stop there, and many travelers would note their stopover in their travel diaries, mentioning the abundance of fresh vegetables and fruit and the quality of the connection with the local population. While the colony and its immediate vicinity were well known, the hinterland remained the domain of the most persistent of dreams. Travelers, cartographers, and utopians would consider it the antechamber of the mythical kingdoms of Congo, Mutapa, and Butua, claiming that the Mountains of the Moon and the source of the Nile were located there. Is there not talk of one of its tributaries, the river Gihon, leading to paradise, and to the kingdom of the Queen of Saba', where the abundant gold mines of King Solomon are located? The Lands of Good Hope had not lost their allure: they revived the fantasies and myths that the Portuguese exploration of the Congo had crushed. In the iconography of the late classical age and the advent of the Age of Enlightenment, the Lands of Good Hope gave rise to an opulent and prosperous Africa that contrasts with the various representations of the Black Continent, its peoples, and its kings as a land left to darkness, whose idolatrous inhabitants are reliant on superstitions and cannibalism to survive. In his *Mémoire sur le pays des Cafres et la terre de Nuyts* (*Dissertation about the Land of the Kaffirs and the Earth of the Nuyts*), published in the early eighteenth century, Jean-Pierre Purry wrote an idyllic description of the Lands of Good Hope to encourage his sovereign to embark on the colonization of these parts. However, it is not until the end of the century that François Levaillant would be entrusted with leading the first expedition to the interior of the southern lands of the Black Continent. Cruelly, this expedition would bring an end to the dreams and fantasies stirred by the idea of colonizing the Lands of Good Hope. Levaillant would cross the hinterland of the Lands of Good Hope, traveling through hostile nature, but would not discover the Mountains of the Moon, the source of the Nile, or the kingdom of the Queen of Saba'.

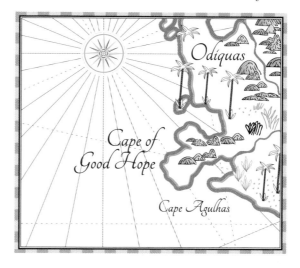

AMERICA

ARAUCANÍA

The Land of Epics

DIEGO DE ALMAGRO, Francisco Pizarro's companion in his conquest of Peru, would be the first to conquer southern Chile as well. In July 1535, Diego de Almagro left the city of Cuzco at the helm of an expedition party of three. After an exhausting trek across the high plateau of the Andes, he crossed the cordillera and entered Chile via the Aconcagua River valley. Almagro threw himself straight into this journey because he had an intuition that this was where to look for the wondrous cities of gold. In vain. Instead of the abundant gold he had hoped for, he found only the remains of plantations cultivated by the Incas a century earlier. After massacring the Indigenous population, adding even more bloodshed to the dark history of the Spanish conquest, Almagro and his three parties returned to Peru by the same route they had come. Pizarro took Almagro as a prisoner and beheaded him shortly after his return, so Pedro de Valdivia took up the baton and set off to complete the conquest of Araucanía, intending to reach the most-southern parts of the continent, from "Valparaiso to the Strait of Magellan." Valdivia dispatched two expeditions to carry out his mission: one on land, the other by sea. The maritime expedition reached "a forest of islands, the Chonos Archipelago, as well as numerous bays and coves," clashed with the Chonos people, and entered along a strait "blocked off by snow-capped peaks, which seemed to be the dark entrance to the Strait of Magellan." Battling the choppy currents until it was no longer able to resist the current, the expedition turned towards Chile "without any other result but the merit of obedience and the reconnaissance of the archipelagos of Chiloé and Chonos." The land expedition ran into the fierce resistance of the Araucanians. The conquest of this region would take three centuries.

While the kingdom of Portugal can boast about its celebrated navigators and explorers in the verses of epic poems or the prose of monumental histories, it is a different matter for Spain. Its conquests became the subject of only one epic, except for one "insignificant" event with regard to its maritime and colonial history: the subjection of the cacique of the Araucanian people, right in Araucanía. The event inspired Alonso de Ercilla to compose the "only heroic and exotic poem of the Spanish Golden Age": *La Araucana*. Because, it must be emphasized, the conquest of Araucanía was nothing like the submission and destruction of the Inca Empire.

Composed between 1569 and 1589, and thus taking twenty years to complete, *La Araucana* recounts the episodes of the heroic resistance the Araucanians mounted against the troops of conquistador Pedro de Valdivia. If the verses from *La Araucana* sound true to life, it is probably because their author participated in the war himself: as legend would have it, he composed the poem's first stanzas on the battlefield. In the tradition of Homer, Virgil, and Lucan, Alonso de Ercilla intended to write a foundational poem. Unusual for his time, Alonso de Ercilla describes the manners, customs, and values of their opponents in detail and praises the courage of these men who defended their native soil with panache and pride.

He excels at painting a picture of battle scenes—with multiple cross-references to the battles of St. Quentin and Lepanto—parades and ceremonies. Like Torquato Tasso in his *Jerusalem Delivered*, and Ludovico Ariosto in his *Orlando furioso*, Ercilla happily blends history with fiction and wonder.

This bleak part of the South American continent would once again ignite the imagination of an eccentric. In 1860, the Frenchman Orélie-Antoine de Tounens, an attorney by trade, traveled deep into Araucanía, where the Indigenous population welcomed him as a liberator and proclaimed him "King of Araucanía and Patagonia." But his reign was short lived. Two years later, the king was forced to leave his kingdom to return to his native Périgord region in France. But the deposed ruler did not admit defeat. He drummed up financial support to save his kingdom and repeatedly returned to reclaim the throne. In vain . . . intercepted each time, he was eventually expelled and forcibly removed by the Chilean authorities to his homeland, where he died in 1878, without being able to reclaim his territory.

Pacific

Ocean

Republic of Chile

Constitución

Co

Chil

San Rafael

Tuce

Concepción

Taleamávida

Lo

Millapoa

San C

Araucanía

Aranco

Angol

Quinchilca

AMERICA

Araucanía

Valdivia

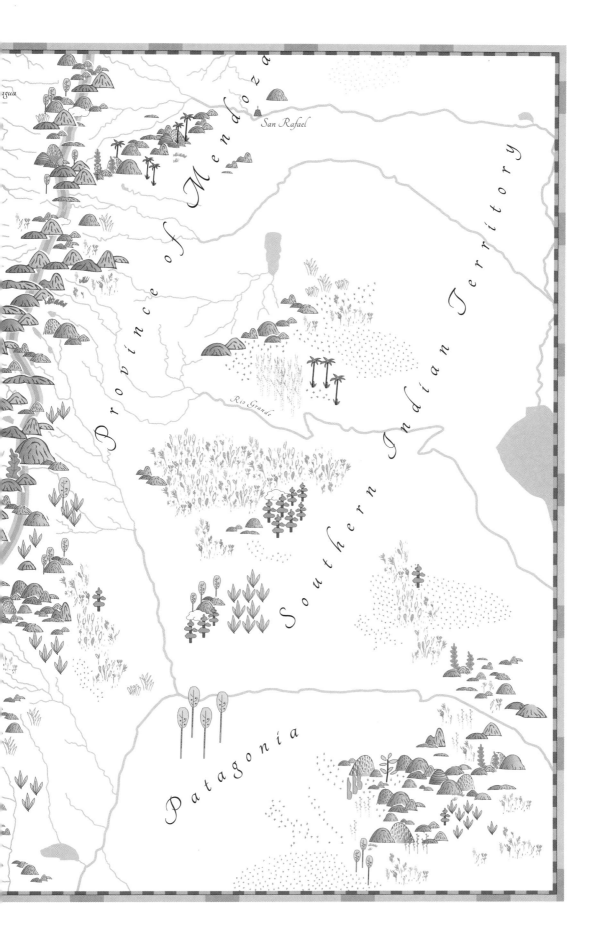

San Rafael

Province of Mendoza

Southern Indian Territory

Rio Grande

Patagonia

CIBOLA

The Country of the Seven Cities

WONDERS, RICHES, RUBIES, but especially gold in abundance . . . that was what Christopher Columbus promised his crew when they sailed under the Spanish flag aboard the *Santa Maria*, the *Pinta*, and the *Niña* to reach the fabulous destinations of India, Cathay, and Cipangu via a route west. He left the port of Palos de la Frontera in 1492. When he reached the West Indies, Christopher Columbus persuaded his men that India was very close. The gold fever that had blinded the sailors' reticence vanished: they had not found the promised riches. What a bitter disappointment! Back in Spain, the Genoese captain did not have the heart to confess his failure to the Catholic king and queen: neither to Isabella, who had backed his operation, nor to Ferdinand, who had followed his royal wife's advice. So he described the golden cities he had dreamed of as if he had actually seen them. So a second expedition was dispatched. It consisted of seventeen ships. Several islands were discovered and explored—but no gold was found. They questioned the Indigenous population. They kept quiet and would pay for their silence with their freedom: hundreds of them became slaves. The spectacle of these chained men revolted the Catholic king and queen. They resolved to put an end to it: Christopher Columbus had lost all credibility. But the Spanish did not give up on the idea of discovering the wonderful cities of gold described by Marco Polo. That is how the myth of the Seven Cities of Cibola was born, whose origins can be traced to Mérida, Spain. Here is how it came about.

In the eighth century, when the Arab leader Musa ibn Nusayr seized the city of Mérida, the capital of Extremadura, the archbishop, six bishops, and their entourage fled, each aboard a ship, by commending their soul and salvation to the Highest. They were determined to save many sacred relics from the hands of the infidels at any cost. After a dangerous sea journey, they are said to have crossed the ocean and reached South America, well before Columbus and the conquistadors. Each one of them is said to have built a city based on justice and fairness, in the wake of the great utopias from Plato to Thomas

Quivíra

San
Sebastián

Boat
Village

N e w

M e x i c o

Sobás

Los Conches

Guadiana

P a c i f i c

Zacatecas

Guadalajara

O c e a n

Îslas
Marías

Mechoacán

Oaxaca

- 1492 -

Cíbola

More. Thanks to the discovery of the continent's riches, most notably gilt metal, these seven cities had prospered.

In 1527, an expedition carried out by Pánfilo de Narváez left Sanlúcar de Barrameda in Spain for the New World. In 1536, only four survivors reached New Spain, present-day Mexico: Alonso del Castillo Maldonado, Andrés Dorantes, Álvar Núñez Cabeza de Vaca—and the Black slave Esteban. The expedition was a disaster. While Cabeza de Vaca described, in a detailed report, the sinking of their ship and its fatal consequences, Esteban's account would grab people's attention, because the slave, basing his report on talk by the Indigenous population, described the existence of several golden cities. One name is repeated several times in his tale: Cibola. The Spaniards were convinced that their expedition had ventured not far from the seven cities founded by the bishops of Mérida.

In 1539, the Franciscan monk Marcos de Niza, convinced to be on the road to the seven cities, sailed to Peru, where he joined Francisco Pizarro in 1530. The lure of the Seven Cities of Gold was not his only obsession, nor did it affect his Christian duties. Denouncing the crimes and abuses Pizarro and his fellow conquistadors had committed, he left for Ecuador, Guatemala, Mexico, and New Mexico, where he lived among the Zuni people. Back in Mexico, he provided a detailed account of his journey in his *Relación . . . a la provincia de Culuacan en Nueva España*, in which he also mentions the existence of the Seven Cities of Gold in Cibola. In his account, he evokes a city larger than Tenochtitlán, whose inhabitants use gold and silver dishes and own pearls, gems, and emeralds.

Viceroy Antonio de Mendoza did not need much more than that to charge Francisco Vásquez de Coronado with heading up an expedition of more than three hundred men to take control of the famous seven cities in 1540. Coronado left Culiacán in April. After several weeks of unsuccessful explorations, Francisco Vásquez de Coronado made Marcos de Niza confess that he had never laid eyes on the cities of gold at all, and that Cibola was but a dream. But the belief in cities made of gold did not falter because of it. The myths of El Dorado, Antillia, the City of the Caesars, or Paititi would soon take over from the Seven Cities of Cibola in capturing the imagination. Nevertheless, Cibola would continue to let readers, travelers, and explorers long for it. Hugo Pratt would give his comic-book hero Corto Maltese the privilege of taking up the baton and heading out in search of Cibola. In the book, the directions to the Seven Cities were inscribed on the skin of a monk, ripped from his body by an Indigenous tribe, and became a relic preserved in the Franciscan convent of the island of San Francesco del Deserto, located in the Venetian Lagoon . . .

Wonders, riches, rubies, and especially gold in abundance . . . That is what Christopher Columbus promised his crew when they sailed under the Spanish flag aboard the Santa Maria, the Pinta, and the Niña to reach the fabulous destination of India via a route west.

EL DORADO

The Golden Kingdom

TOGETHER WITH PAÏTITI and the Seven Cities of Cibola, El Dorado is one of the great mythical lands sought by the Spanish conquistadors. The mountains and cities of gold described in splendid detail by Christopher Columbus on his return from his first expedition captured the imagination of all, travelers and historians alike. Among the latter were Francisco López de Gómara and Sebastián Garcilaso de la Vega, who hypothesized that upon the arrival of the Spanish, the last Incas must have fled and taken all their wealth with them. They would then have founded a new kingdom in the Southeast of the continent: Paititi, with its capital Manoa.

In 1534, Captain Sebastián de Belalcázar, one of Francisco Pizarro's second officers in the bloody conquest of New Granada and Peru, seized the Inca city of Quito. In search of Paititi and the fabulous cities of gold, he listened with interest to an amazing story by the Indigenous people: on the Day of the Sun, the Great Inca would immerse himself completely in a sea of gold, a ritual that would bestow upon him the name "the Golden One." This custom is not made up. Each year, the cacique of the Chibchas people would be anointed with oil and fragrant scents, covered with gold powder, and plunged into the lake while the members of his tribe would throw gold objects into the water. The name "golden," which the Spaniards translated literally into "El Dorado," hence first referred to the person they imagined to be an Inca sovereign or a high priest, before designating the famous golden sea in which he was submerged. This sea really exists: it is Lake Parime. The conquistadors imagined it to be full of gold, before attributing this fabulous feature to the entire kingdom.

On the basis of Indigenous people's testimonies, Sebastián de Belalcázar began to search for the kingdom of El Dorado, not in the Southeast of the continent, but in the North. He founded Santiago de Cali in 1536 and the cities of Pasto and Popayán in 1537. El Dorado remains hidden to this day.

But the myth did not fade so easily. Many explorers threw themselves into this adventure. Among them was Francisco de Orellana, who traveled downstream on the Río Napo, the Río Negro, and then the Amazon, covering more than 3,000 miles (nearly 5,000 kilometers). All of them would travel up and down the South American continent, searching far and wide for the Golden Kingdom. With the missionary Gaspar de Carvajal's publication of Orellana's travel diary, the myth that crossed over with that of the Seven Cities of Cibola met with a great echo among the conquistadors. They found hope again.

On the Day of the Sun, the Great Inca would immerse himself completely in a sea of gold, a ritual that would bestow upon him the name "the Golden One."

El Dorado was eventually located somewhere between the Orinoco River and the Amazon, across the present-day territories of Brazil, Venezuela, and Guyana. Throughout the sixteenth century, countless expeditions were dispatched from all Spanish cities founded on the continent to finally fully explore it—all of them ended in fiasco. The location of the kingdom where gold flowed remained unknown. But what did it matter?! Failing to find the country, the conquistadors searched for the lake. But without much success either. On maps and in the imagination of explorers, however, one constant remained: El Dorado must be located in the North of the South American continent. Explorer Walter Raleigh embarked on his own journey in search of the lost kingdom, appointed by Queen Elizabeth I of England. In *The Discovery of the Large, Rich, and Beautiful Empire of Guiana, with a Relation of the Great and Golden City of Manoa* (which the Spaniards call El Dorado), an account of his 1595 journey, he wrote: "Many years since I had knowledge, by relation, of that mighty, rich, and beautiful empire of Guiana, and of that great and golden city,

which the Spaniards call El Dorado, and the naturals Manoa." But much like his predecessors, Walter Raleigh would not discover the Golden Kingdom either. His idyllic description of Guyana, however, convinced the queen not to put a stop to the English exploration endeavors. Although it had not been discovered, El Dorado would become one of the regions of choice for utopians in the classical age. It inspired the well-written pages of François Fénelon and Denis Vairasse. And although upon his return back upstream the Amazon in the years 1743 to 1744, the French naturalist Charles-Marie de La Condamine intended to kill off, once and for all, the myth, by claiming that neither the golden city of Manoa nor a kingdom entirely made of gold was situated anywhere near the Amazon River or Lake Parime, El Dorado would continue to fascinate, inspiring two chapters in Voltaire's *Candide.* There are long passages relating to the conquest of Peru in the French writer's monumental *An Essay on Universal History, the Manners, and Spirit of Nations* (translated by Thomas Nugent).

Corto Maltese, the hero created by Hugo Pratt, follows in the footsteps of yet another explorer also in search of the fabulous disappeared kingdom. Having expressed his doubts to his companion Jeremiah Steiner, he says: "Just to find what others have not found . . . the El Dorado . . . the Golden Man . . . the legend of this continent."

THE LAND OF THE AMAZONS

WHO ARE THE AMAZONS? These splendid and fearsome creatures have a long history. In his *Histories*, Herodotus reports that the Scythians called them oiorpata: "killers of men." While hypotheses vary as to the etymology of the name "Amazon," all ancient accounts and descriptions agree on their being formidable warriors devoted entirely to the art of war, to the point of using men only for the purpose of perpetuating the female race. "And as for their children," Diodorus of Sicily recounts, "they mutilated both the legs and the arms of the males, incapacitating them in this way for the demands of war, and in the case of the females they seared the right breast that it might not project when their bodies matured and be in the way" (translated by Charles Henry Oldfather).

The location of the land of the Amazons would shift over time. It was apparently in Libya, where they would dominate over the Atlantians, the Numidians, and the Ethiopians, that the Amazons would first impose their law, before migrating to Colchis, and before settling on the shores of the Thermodon River, from where they would subjugate neighboring peoples. Their leader, who called herself the daughter of Ares, would eventually be defeated by Hercules. Euripides writes about the hero's glorious campaign in the following words in his play *Heracles*: "Then he gathered friends from all over Greece and fought the mounted army of the Amazons who lived round the lake Maeotis, a lake fed by many rivers, beyond the Euxeine Sea. They took from their barbarian queen, Hippolyta, the golden girdle—a deadly labour!—and this glorious spoil of war they brought back to Greece, where it is safe in Mycenae" (translated by George Theodoridis). For Herodotus, the residence of the Amazons was located at the edge of the known world, on the shores of the Euxine Sea. As the myth traveled throughout history, Arrian reports that the Macedonian prince Alexander met them before marrying their queen. Diodorus gives some credit to this fable, yet many historians refute it, including Plutarch, in his *Life of Alexander*. Throughout the Middle Ages, the Amazons continued to exert their powerful fascination over historians, geographers, and cosmographers alike. Their territory, called "Amazonia," or "Feminye," combined all the attributes of a utopia. Marco Polo and Christopher Columbus, making the myth their own, each evoked the "Islands of Women." And the Venetian confirmed that there were two islands on the edge of India, "called Male and Female": "The people . . . are very reserved in their intercourse with their wives. All the latter, indeed, dwell in another isle which is called Female" (translated by Hugh Murray). The etymology of their name, the functions assigned to men, and the fate awaiting newborns all became the subject of numerous prognostications and debates. But all agreed that the Amazons were fearless horsewomen, skillful huntresses, and distinguished warriors. From the three known worlds, the myth of the Amazons spread to the fourth, thanks to the explorer Francisco de Orellana. Gaspar de Carvajal, the Franciscan monk who accompanied him, kept a journal of the expedition. He reports that after sailing downstream the Río Negro, the explorer and his men had entered a wider river, where they were attacked by valiant and belligerent female fighters. Since they noticed no men among the attackers, Orellana reportedly identified these warriors as the Amazons. He would naturally give the same name to the river itself. Looking for gold everywhere, a few conquistadors, having failed to discover Paititi, El Dorado, and the Seven Cities of Cibola, got it in their heads that the Amazons were guarding the gold. What other reason would there be for them to so fiercely defend their territory from men? In *The New Found World, or Antarctike*, the cosmographer André Thevet uses the following words to denounce their cruelty: "They make warre ordinarily against some other nation. And those whom they take in the warre, they vse most cruelly and inhumainely for to make them die, they hang them by one leg on a trée, and leauing them after this sort, they goe their wayes, and if it happen that they be not dead, when they returne, they will shoote at them aboue ten thousande times, but they eate them not as others doe, but they burne them vntill they be consumed to ashes" (translated by Thomas Hacket). The myth of the ruthless women warriors would persist,

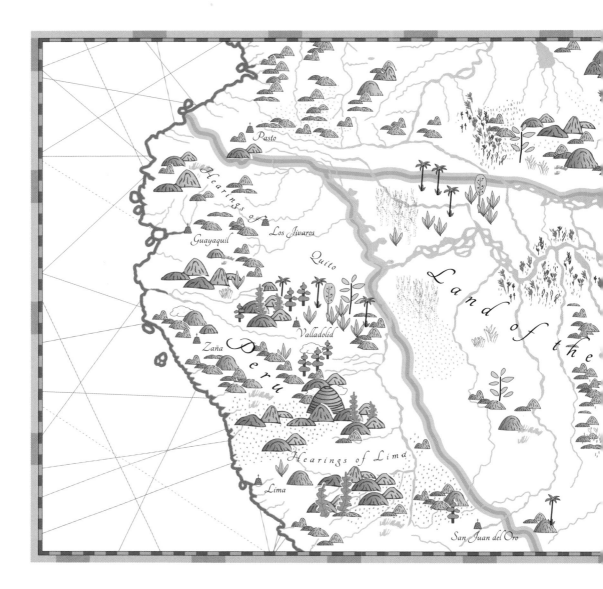

but their kingdom remained impossible to locate, so many seventeenth-century adventurers ventured to seek it. In vain . . . between 1743 and 1744, the French naturalist Charles-Marie de La Condamine traveled downstream the Amazon River. It is no surprise that he found no trace of the belligerent women soldiers. His *Voyage de la rivière des Amazones* (*Journey along the River of the Amazons*) put a real stop to the ravings of Spanish and British explorers who

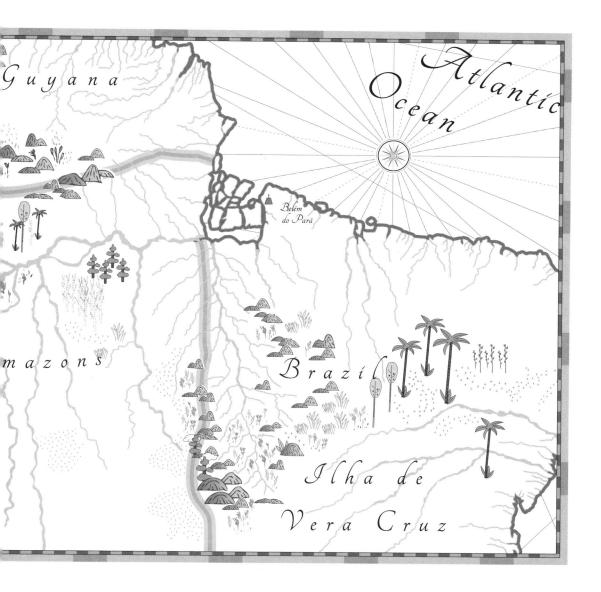

had come to find surviving remnants of the ancient matriarchal society of the Amazons at the river basin. For a long time, however, on maps and globes and in iconology, America would be depicted as a beautiful, bare-breasted woman carrying a quiver and arrows, watching over the Amazon and aiming at the conquerors, conquistadors, and other unscrupulous temple looters as a warning.

TIERRA DEL FUEGO

A Labyrinth of Fjords, Reefs, and Pitfalls

TO REACH THE MOLUCCAS and its many fragrant spices—in particular cloves, which were very popular in the kitchens and on the dining tables of royal courts—Ferdinand Magellan set off for this archipelago by taking the route west. In August 1519, at the head of five carracks, he left Seville. After a brief stop in the Canary Islands, the fleet arrived in the waters off the Brazilian coast in December and put down anchor in the bay of Santa Lucia, now Rio de Janeiro. They resumed their course and set sail for the south to circumnavigate the continent and reach the Moluccas.

The farther south they traveled, the colder it got. Magellan decided to overwinter his crew in the estuary of San Julián. Disagreeing with their risk-taking commander's judgment, three of his captains, Juan de Cartagena, Luis de Mendoza, and Gaspar de Quesada, started a mutiny that was quickly curbed by Magellan, thanks to the support of the sailors who had remained loyal to him. To locate a passage allowing them to come out on the other side of the continent, Magellan sent one of his carracks on reconnaissance: the Santiago. But the ship sank, and with it all bodies and goods aboard.

Magellan then decided to go himself in search of the famous passage, heading the rest of the fleet. At the end of October, they entered a strait that Magellan would call "Estrecho de todos los Santos" ("Strait of All Saints"), which would later be renamed in his honor. It is a veritable labyrinth of fjords and reefs lined by steep cliffs and craggy coastlines. On several occasions, while crossing the channel during ice-cold nights, sailors perceived great fires on land with thick curls of smoke emanating from them.

The land would therefore initially be named "Tierra del Humo" ("Land of Smoke") before receiving the designation "Tierra del Fuego" ("Land of Fire"). But what is this land exactly? An island? An archipelago? A promontory?

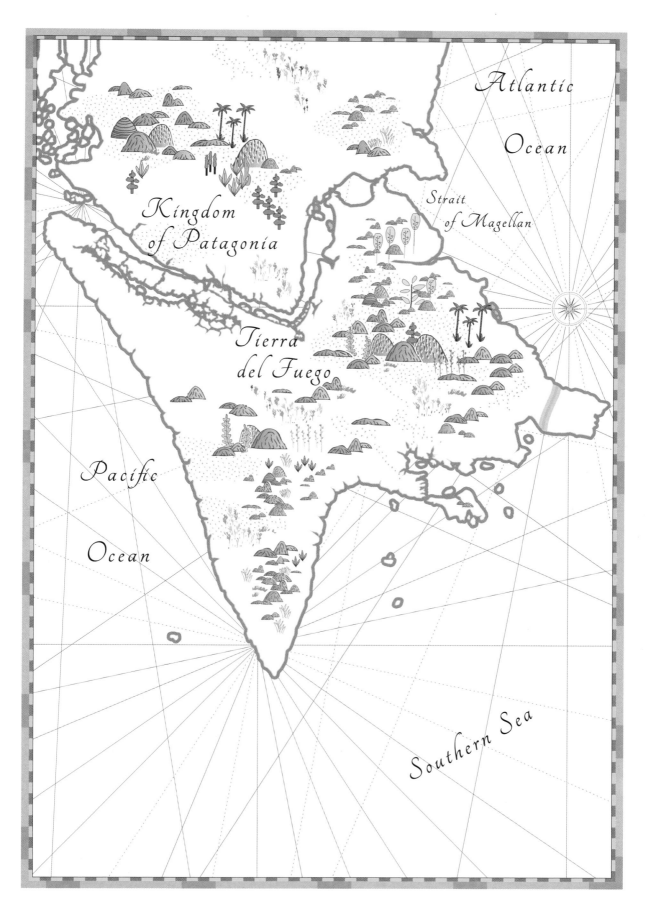

Ferdinand Magellan, who was busy carrying out his mission, did not care: he would continue on his way, no matter what, eventually arriving at the other end of the strait. In the vastness of the ocean and with Olympian calm, he headed west. Alas, a few months later, on a beach in the Philippines, Magellan would be speared to death by Indigenous tribes. Of the proud expedition, only one ship with nineteen sailors aboard would manage to return to Spain. Shortly after his return, King Charles V armed another fleet of six carracks and sent it on the route opened up by Magellan. Although they did not encounter any obstacles crossing the Atlantic, the fate of the carracks varied once they entered the infernal strait: several were damaged, one was sunk, and another was lost. Four of them, albeit with great difficulty, managed to sail along the strait. In the darkness of night, the men saw fires on both shores; spotted a canoe, whalebones, and a harpoon; and then made out a human presence. "These Indians would ignite firebrands, and some of us thought they were about to set fire to the ships. They did not dare come closer, and we were unable to pursue them in a rowing boat because they were ahead of us in their canoes." The ships continued on their route, but, again, only one would return safely.

In 1534, another expedition was dispatched. The Land of Fire was set on bringing bad luck. During a stop to go ashore before the strait, a famine broke out, followed by a mutiny. The survivors found refuge in Brazil "after having eaten the leather tying the masts' yards." Despite the witness accounts by survivors of these three expeditions, Tierra del Fuego remained an enigma. Some argued that there was a continent south of the strait, a hypothesis defended by the German cartographer Johannes Schöner. For nearly half a century, the Spanish Crown sent ever more expeditions on reconnaissance and to map the strait—as well as to block access for foreign ships.

In 1581, an armada consisting of twenty-five ships left the Spanish coast to found a colony in Tierra del Fuego. It took more than two years of ups and downs, shipwrecks, wanderings, and losses for the first three hundred settlers of the strait to set foot on the desolate soil of the Land of Fire. After having laid the foundations for a first city, Nombre de Jesús, where some of them would stay, the settlers made for a more sheltered place, which it would take tremendous effort to reach. They wanted to found a colony, which they called Ciudad del Rey Felipe. Destiny was to be cruel to the settlers of both cities. Isolated in a hostile landscape, and

> Despite the witness accounts by survivors, Tierra del Fuego remained an enigma.

able to rely on only what the sea supplied, the settlers withered away. Those who tried to leave the cities behind in makeshift boats, handing over their salvation to the Highest, would sink in one of the strait's bends. When, in 1586, the twenty survivors of Ciudad del Rey Felipe had managed to return to Nombre de Jesús on foot, their trek was lined with the corpses of two hundred of those they had left behind.

In the bay of Nombre de Jesús, where all settlers had found their death, the three ships of the privateer Thomas Cavendish had anchored. Cavendish offered to take the unfortunate survivors to Peru, but only one accepted. The others would die in Nombre de Jesús, abandoned by all, including their Lord. In Ciudad del Rey Felipe, Cavendish, measuring the magnitude of the disaster on the basis of the corpses of these men "who died like dogs," renamed the bay Port Famine. It still bears this name to this day, offering to the gusts the relics of what was meant to become the most modern, the most splendid, and the most sumptuous of the cities of the New World.

SOUTHERN
LANDS

NEW CYTHERA

Paradise on Earth

AFTER A LONG STAY of three and a half months in Montevideo, La Boudeuse and L'Étoile crossed the Strait of Magellan, got through to the Pacific, and laid anchor off an enchanting and Edenic island. In the first volume of his journals, Louis-Antoine de Bougainville, sent by Louis XVI to explore the Pacific Ocean to discover new lands, writes about coming across this undiscovered island. But the island was not unknown. It had been "discovered" a year earlier by the British navigator Samuel Wallis, who was heading a ship sent to observe the passage of Venus, and who baptized it in honor of his sovereign King George Island. Recalling reading François Fénelon's *The Adventures of Telemachus*, notably the episode about the hero blaming the excesses of the inhabitants of the island of Kythira, the island of love and desire, Bougainville proudly commented on his "discovery" and writes: "And so I have named it New Cythera, and the protection of Minerva is as necessary here as in the ancient Cythera to defend one against the influence both of the climate and of the people's morals." On this island, the manners and customs of the inhabitants, the navigator and his men are reminded, are not unlike those of the mythical island of Kythira. Indeed, the climate here is mild and temperate, the air and the skies are of absolute purity, and the soil and the trees produce fruit in abundance. "The products we saw," the navigator notes, "consist of coconuts, bananas, yams, sugar cane, various other fruits and vegetables, a kind of wild indigo, various other fruits and vegetables [*sic*], and black, yellow, and red dye." The inhabitants are very tall: 6 to 6.5 feet tall, both men and women. But most strange of all, they are white and of good blood. All are beautiful. Their teeth are white, their features delicate and regular, their hair silky, be it black, brown, blond . . . or red. Their spiritual qualities are commensurate with their physical beauty: they are good people, affable and generous. Their manners, in harmony with the climate, are simple and gentle. "The character of the nation has appeared mild and beneficent to us," Bougainville continues. "Though the isle is divided into many little districts, each of which has its own master, yet there does not seem to be any civil war, or any private hatred in the isle. It is probably that the people of Taiti

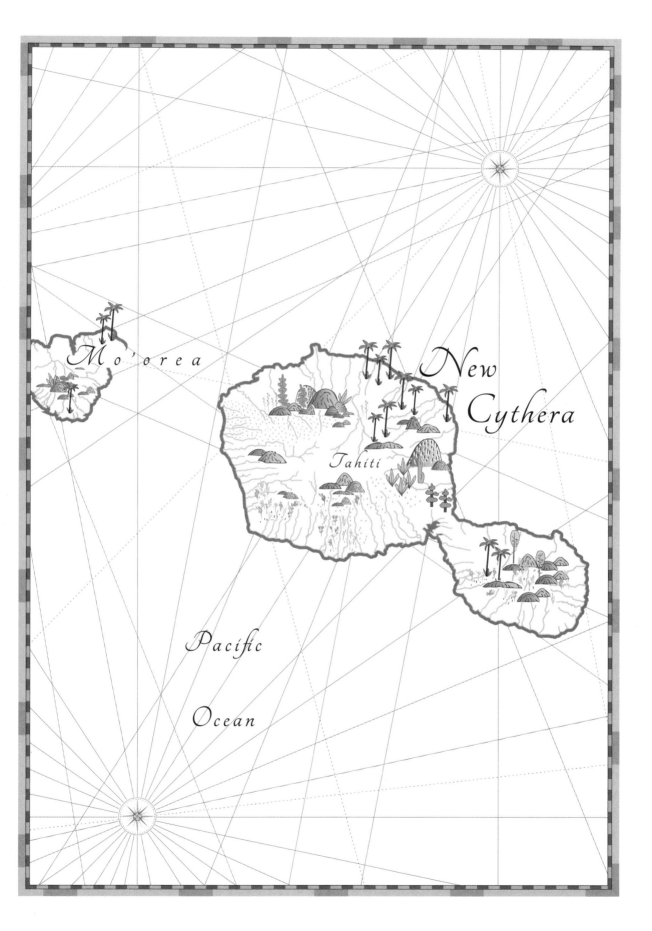

Mo'orea

New
Cythera

Tahiti

Pacific

Ocean

deal amongst each other with unquestioned sincerity. Whether they be at home or no, by day or by night, their houses are always open. Every one gathers fruits from the first tree he meets with, or takes some in any house into which he enters. It should seem as if, in regard to things absolutely necessary for the maintenance of life, there was no personal property amongst them, and that they all had an equal right to those articles." "Everything is for all," as philosopher Denis Diderot would later write in his *Addendum to the Journey of Bougainville*.

The sailors in particular fell for the charms of these attractive women. The naturalist Philibert Commerson writes in his letter *Sur la découverte de la Nouvelle Île de Cythère ou Taïti* (*On the Discovery of the New Island of Cythera or Tahiti*): "Born under the most beautiful sky, fed by the fruit of a land that is fertile without being cultivated, governed by the fathers of the family rather than by kings, they recognize no God other than Love; every day is dedicated to it, the whole island is its temple, all women are idolaters, all men worship it. And what women they are! They rival the Georgians in beauty, and the three Graces without their veils." The islanders do not know indecency and, willingly yielding to their desires, mate freely and joyfully in the face of heaven and Earth. On this subject, Commerson writes: "The act of creating one's kind is an act of religion; its preludes are encouraged by the vows and songs of all assembled people, and the end is celebrated with universal applause; every stranger is allowed to participate in these happy mysteries; it is even one of the duties of hospitality to invite them." Bougainville also struggles to exactly comprehend their beliefs and religion. "We have seen wooden statues among them, which we took for idols; but how did they worship them?" he wondered.

A stubborn desire to indulge in love and pleasure, gentle superstitions, a mode of government based on harmony, giving oneself over entirely to the generosity and the luxuriousness of the island . . . might Bougainville and his men have arrived in paradise on Earth? Is this Eden, sought by so many travelers and situated in so many different places by the ancient Greeks, possibly located on an island in the Pacific? A "modern Jason," Bougainville would be held for a schemer, a daredevil, and a feather worker. The English navigator Alexander Dalrymple would write harshly in his *Voyages*: "Bougainville, who was ambitious about female suffrage, forgot what he had left behind for so long, and hurried back to entertain Europeans with his stories of the delights of New Cythera."

The inhabitants are very tall: six, to six and a half feet tall, both men and women. But most strange of all, they are White and of good blood. All are beautiful. Their teeth are white, their features delicate and regular, their hair silky, be it black, brown, blond ... or red.

TERRA AUSTRALIS

OF ALL THE MYTHICAL LANDS that were invented before being discovered, Terra Australis is probably the one that led to the greatest amount of speculation. To counterbalance the northern lands, ancient cosmologists postulated the existence of a land beyond the torrid zone with equal landmass to the territories of the North: the Antichthone. Not knowing whether it was inhabited or even habitable, they nonetheless considered it large enough to deserve to be labeled a continent.

In a fictitious dialogue written after the *Philippics* by Aelianus, Theopompus of Chios mentions the existence of a continent down under, situated beyond the edges of the known world. The Machimoi, a warrior class, apparently live there in perpetual war against the Eusebes, the peaceful beings. In his dialogue, Europe, Africa, and Asia are presented as islands surrounding the great ocean: the antipodean land is depicted as the only continent.

In the fourth century BCE, Euhemerus recounts in his *Sacred History* his fabulous journey to the island of Panchaea, on the eastern edges of the ecumene. The sublime geometry of the city of Panchaea reflects the perfection of its institutions and the moral accomplishment of its inhabitants, who are divided into three equal classes. According to Euhemerus, Panchaea owed its perfection to its total absence of contact with the known world.

Diodorus of Sicily describes the City of the Sun evoked by Iambulus in his account of his travels through the Indian Ocean. After four months aboard, Iambulus and his companion reached the Island of the Sun, a disc with a circumference of 5,000 stades. Its inhabitants, the Children of the Sun—so named because they worshiped the Sun King—are of remarkable beauty and nobility, and their voice box allowed them to hold two conversations at once. After seven years spent in this city, Iambulus and his companion, considered imperfect, were eventually banished. Iambulus returned to the known world after four more months of traveling.

In *A True Story*, Lucian also gave rise to a southern utopia, but for the sake of parody and satire and to make a mockery of the genre. He opens his story with the following words: "I

write of matters which I neither saw nor suffered, nor heard by report from others, which are in no being, nor possible ever to have a beginning. Let no man therefore in any case give any credit to them" (translated by Francis Hickes). After a storm that capsized the ship, the travelers land on a floating island, where they are greeted by Hippogypians. They win a battle alongside the king of the island, Endymion, against Phaethon, the king of a neighboring island. After many adventures, the travelers reach an island floating in a sea of milk. Rhadamanthus, the reigning king, points out the path they need to follow to reach the famous southern continent: "When you are past these [islands], you shall come into the great continent, over against your own country, where you shall suffer many afflictions, and pass through many nations, and meet with men of inhuman conditions, and at length attain to the other continent."

Its inhabitants, the Children of the Sun—so named because they worshiped the Sun King—are of admirable beauty and nobility.

The utopian tradition of the ancient Greeks, and the existence of a southern continent itself, will be strongly criticized by Origen, Lactantius, and Augustine of Hippo. The Church Fathers would not accept the mention of a land that was not named in the Bible, and were confirmed in their opinion by Ptolemy. At the same time, however, many scholars continued to assert its existence. Pierre d'Ailly confirmed it in his *Imago Mundi* in 1410. However, the circumnavigation of Africa by the Portuguese in the late fifteenth century and the discovery of a fourth world eventually pushed back the margins of the known world and would make the existence of a southern continent possible again.

In the sixteenth century, the southern continent appeared as a huge landmass on Oronce Finé's and Mercator's world maps and took the form of the island of "Great Java," which had featured on the maps of the geographers of Dieppe.

While travelers such as Nicolas Durand de Villegagnon, Jean de Léry, and André Thevet believed they had discovered this famous land, giving it names such as "Southern Indies" or "French Antarctica," people such as Thomas More in his *Utopia* from 1516, François Rabelais in his *Pantagruel* from 1532, Joseph Hall in his *Mundus alter et idem* from 1605, and, above all, Gabriel de Foigny with *The Southern Land, Known* from 1676 and Denis Vairasse with his *History of Sevarambes*, published between 1677 and 1679, continued the utopian fantasies about the southern continent by writing fictitious travel accounts set in idealized destinations.

The Dutch navigators' discoveries of New Guinea, the Solomon Islands, and then Van Diemen's Land (Tasmania) and Staten Land (New Zealand) in the Indian Ocean revived the myth of this continent before it was located ever farther south, toward those areas of the globe that had been left out of world maps.

In the eighteenth century, the navigators Samuel Wallis, James Cook, and Louis-Antoine de Bougainville were dispatched by their respective nations, predominantly to explore the South Sea and discover this famous southern continent. Australia and New Zealand, which were discovered through these explorations, were neither utopias nor ideal worlds and thus temporarily put an end to the myth of the southern continent. These trips did not prove in vain for the imagination, however, because the "discovery" of Tahiti gave rise to another myth that would blossom in its own right: that of New Cythera.

THE EDGE OF THE WORLD

THE ISLES OF THE BLESSED

Apart from the World and Its People

IN ANCIENT TIMES, there were islands of which it was said that they welcomed those who had stood out during their earthly existence for the righteousness of their actions: these are the Isles of the Blessed. Plato in his *Gorgias* and Hesiod in his *Theogony* situated them in the Oceanus River, at the world's western edge, in the kingdom of Cronus, the land of the night sun.

Other authors placed them in the vicinity of the Elysian Plain. In his *Threnos*, Pindar describes life on these islands in the following terms: "For them, beneath us while the night is here, | There blazes down the power of the sun; | In fields crimson with roses | They have their suburbs, with their shady trees | Of frankincense . . ., and other trees | Weighted with golden fruit. | Some take delight in horses, some | In exercises, some in games of draughts, | Others in the music of lyres, | And happiness is common to them all | In its full bloom, completely" (translated by Marianne McDonald). In his *Olympian Odes*, the poet writes further: "But having the sun always in equal nights and equal days, the good receive a life free from toil, not scraping with the strength of their arms the earth, nor the water of the sea, for the sake of a poor sustenance. But in the presence of the honored gods, those who gladly kept their oaths enjoy a life without tears, while the others undergo a toil that is unbearable to look at. Those who have persevered three times, on either side, to keep their souls free from all wrongdoing, follow Zeus' road to the end, to the tower of Cronus, where ocean breezes blow around the island of the blessed, and flowers of gold are blazing, some from splendid trees on land, while water nurtures others" (translated by Diane Arnson Svarlien). Away from the world, from the cities and humankind, the Isles of the Blessed were for the Greeks the "new city" that Plato wished for and announced in his *Laws*. In mythology, the Isle of the Blessed is also Leuce, known as the White Isle as well. Located in the Euxine Sea, at the mouth of the Ister River, it is one of the gates to Hades guarded by the shadows of Achilles and Helen.

THE GARDEN OF THE HESPERIDES

The Apples of Discord

WHERE IS THE FAMOUS Garden of the Hesperides? Like many mythical places, its location fluctuates and is at the whim of writings and eras. The Greek thinker Strabo in his *Geographica* and the Greek lyric poet Stesichorus place the Garden of the Hesperides not far from the city of Tartessos, in the southwest of the Iberian Peninsula. Some authors situate it at the heart of the Fortunate Isles. Others believe to recognize it in the mountains of Arcadia, at the center of the Peloponnese Peninsula, or on the edge of the Aegean Sea. For Apollodorus of Rhodes, the mythical garden lies among the Hyperboreans in the Atlas Mountains. Diodorus of Sicily perceived it on Hespera, an island of Lake Tritonia, in Cyrenaica—not far from the Amazons of Libya.

"We are told, namely, that there was once on the western parts of Libya, on the bounds of the inhabited world, a race which was ruled by women," he writes about the Amazons in his *Library of History* (translated by Charles Henry Oldfather). "Now there have been in Libya a number of races of women who were warlike and greatly admired for their manly vigour; for instance, tradition tells us of the race of the Gorgons. . . . As mythology relates, [the Amazons'] home was on an island which, because it was in the west, was called Hespera, and it lay in the marsh Tritonis. This marsh was near the ocean which surrounds the earth and received its name from a certain river Triton which emptied into it; and this marsh was also near Ethiopia and that mountain by the shore of the ocean which is the highest of those in the vicinity and impinges upon the ocean and is called by the Greeks Atlas. The island mentioned above was of great size and full of fruit-bearing trees of every kind . . . and possessed a multitude of the precious stones which the Greeks call anthrax, sardion, and smaragdos."

As their name, deriving from "evening," suggests, the Hesperides return at the end of the day, at twilight, at the fall of night. They are the guardians of the gates that separate the day from the night and the night from the day. Metaphorically speaking, they also watch over the portals separating life and death. The Hesperides are young virgins with crystalline voices. In his

The Hesperides, these young virgins, guard the golden apples that were coveted by many and are at the source of the Trojan War.

Theogony, Hesiod speaks of them as the women of the "dark of night." They are warriors who, like the Amazons, shunned the company of men—which is why the ancient Greeks called them "the Amazons of Libya." They come in groups of three and are linked to two other female trinities: the Keres, also known as the daughters of Nyx and related to the Furies, and the Moirai, who pull the threads that each represent the life of a mortal, and that, if they break, result in a person's demise. They are the ones who, if we believe the many traditions, guard the golden apples that were coveted by many and are at the source of the Trojan War. Let's recall the mythical episode: The ruler of Argos, Eurystheus, convinces Hercules to pick the golden apples from the Garden of the Hesperides. But Hercules does not know where the garden was. So he goes to the shore of the Eridanos River to the Illyrians. The river nymphs show him the place where the primitive sea god Nereus, the "Old Man of the Sea," sleeps. Hercules manages to capture him and forces him to reveal the location of the fabulous garden. To escape the hero's embrace, Nereus gives him directions for the long and treacherous path.

Leaving behind Libya, Hercules is forced to confront and challenge the giant Antaeus, who draws his force from the earth. Hercules snubs him out by lifting him and crushing him. Hercules travels across the fabulous African continent recounted by the ancient Greeks to find the garden: the land of the Pygmies, whom he defeats, that of king Busiris and his son Amphidamas. Then he reaches Asia. And finally Arabia, where he faces and kills Emathion, one of the sons of Eos and the goddess Aurora. Aboard a golden boat, he rocks across the sea and fights off the eagle that, in the Caucasus Mountains, is devouring Prometheus's liver. Prometheus, grateful to Hercules, recommends that he ask the giant Atlas to harvest three golden apples for him. Hercules achieves this by offering the giant to support the weight of the heavens for him. Atlas accepts, goes to pick the apples, and returns to Hercules. However, having tasted freedom, the giant refuses to return to his place. The cunning Hercules then asks him to hold the heavens just briefly while he adjusts his headband. Atlas accepts and puts down the apples so Hercules can retie his headband. Once released from the weight, Hercules abandons the gullible Atlas, grabs the apples, and returns to Eurystheus.

According to another version of the myth, Hercules reaches the Garden of the Hesperides after a long journey, and its entrance is guarded by the dragon Ladon. Hercules kills it with his arrows and grabs the apples. Then, the poet Apollodore recounts, "He brought them to Eurysthée, who gave them to the hero himself. Heraclès then gave them to Athena, but the goddess returned them to the Hesperides, because it was not allowed, by divine law, that the apples were placed somewhere" (translated by James George Frazer).

Wherever and how they were picked—and by whom—the golden apples of the Garden of the Hesperides would traditionally become a symbol of squabbling and disaster. In *The Abduction of Helen*, the Greek poet Colouthus recounts the anger of Iris, who, furious at not having been invited to the wedding party of Peleus and Thetis, throws the apple onto the guests' table, which will eventually sow discord among the goddesses—and start a war. Her ploy worked beyond her expectations: step by step, bewitched by the apple thrown to the lionesses, Hera and Aphrodite would tear each other to pieces. And it is yet another one of the apples of this famous garden that the young Paris chose to offer to the goddess Aphrodite to obtain Helen, who would be at the center of the Trojan War and inspire Homer's two famous poems: the *Iliad* and the *Odyssey*.

LEMURIA

A Lost World

IN THE NINETEENTH CENTURY, the zoologist Philip Sclater wrote that at the origin of all the other continents there was one single one, which he named after a species of Malagasy monkeys: Lemuria. Following in his footsteps, several scholars repeated this hypothesis, naming this continent Lemuria, or Mu. For all of them, this continent was not just the origin of the inhabited world, but also the source of science and the arts. Apparently, the scientists who had lived there had recorded everything on tablets when a great cataclysm swallowed up the continent in 12,000 BCE. To find the vestiges of this place, Walter Scott-Elliot and James Churchward spent years sailing to and fro across the Pacific and the Indian Oceans. Through their search, they ended up finding signs, marks, and symbols that the extraordinary inhabitants of this primitive continent had left behind, and of which the Moai of Easter Island are the most amazing remains. Inspired by theories developed by Scott-Elliot, Churchward, and Helena Blavatsky, Jules Hermann, a scholar from Réunion, reinterpreted the myth of the lost continent in his own way. He explained the original configuration of this unique continent made up of Africa and engulfed lands, of which only the peaks that form the Mascarene Islands emerge from the sea: Mauritius and Réunion. According to his treatise *Révélations du Grand Océan* (*Revelations of the Great Ocean*), Lemuria was populated by giants, the Lemurians, who, in addition to science and the arts, had invented a perfect language that they had slowly spread almost everywhere across the globe before the great cataclysm happened. To support his theories, he tried to re-create this language and proposed to explain how it worked. But above all, he turned the Lemurians into the ancestors of Europeans. In these giants, he recognized "this oceanic race from which the first Europeans derived." Jules Hermann was so invested in seeing these distant relatives as the ancestors of Europeans because he was unconsciously trying to get closer to this faraway Europe that made him dream. Crossing fables, legends, and myths associated with Atlantis and Mu, Lemuria would continue to fascinate and make travelers and writers dream, inspiring several of them to some of their most beautiful reveries.

THULE

The Land of Nowhere

PYTHEAS COULD NOT BELIEVE his own eyes. The island in front of him did not look like any other natural landscape. He would name it Thule. The indefinable landscape seemed to oscillate between liquid and solid states. Submerged in the freezing mist, the island of Thule had nothing in common with what explorers from the Mediterranean world had ever encountered.

Pytheas, who had sailed from Massalia (present-day Marseille) aboard the fragile *Kyteria* to explore the northern oceans, had already discovered more than needed to shake up the common sense of his time. He crossed the Pillars of Hercules, which the ancient Greeks considered the outer gate of civilization. He then made for the North, passing around the Gironde estuary. Fascinated by it, he discovered the mechanism of tides, which he quickly associated with the lunar cycle. Past the island of Ushant, he made surprisingly accurate measurements of the coasts of Britain. His calculations, drawn up some 2,300 years ago, are of extraordinary precision.

But it was six days after leaving the coast of Great Britain, heading north, that he would discover the famous island. It was as if day and night were abolished here: the sun described a discrete sine curve on the ground. A brilliant scientific mind, Pytheas would be the first to explain the midnight sun.

In his book *On the Ocean*, he described this amazing island that appeared to him following Strabo as a "marine lung." Neither land nor ocean. Bathed in the sun that seemed unwilling to rise above the horizon, Thule defined a new frontier for the visible world.

The Greek commentators on Pytheas had sharp teeth. For many, he was just a storyteller. Neither Strabo nor Polybius took him seriously. The ancient Greeks knew very little about the northern seas. In the second century BCE, Ptolemy and Hipparchus got embroiled in speculations about Thule's real location, which only one of their people had claimed to have encountered. Tacitus, recalling the testimony of explorer Agricola, located it near Scotland.

Bathed in the sun that seemed unwilling to rise above the horizon, Thule defined a new frontier for the visible world.

Procopius of Caesarea, in the sixth century, interpreted it as Norway; five hundred years later, Adam of Bremen identified it as Iceland.

If one is to follow Pytheas's description, the term "marine lung" evokes the consistency of jellyfish. Scientists are aware of this phenomenon that accompanies the transformation of water into ice. The sea then takes on a moving and viscous aspect, which may well be at the source of the explorer's description and could locate the legendary island near Greenland, or between Scandinavia, Iceland, and Scotland—in the Faroe Islands archipelago.

In the seventeenth century, cartographer Joan Blaeu would do away with all the guesswork and leave an empty space at the island's presumed site.

The many different quotations and assumptions that punctuate ancient writings help ensure the vitality of the myth of Thule. And in the imagination of navigators, cartographers, and cosmographers, Thule would long remain the endpoint of the edge of the world, the island of perpetual darkness, of harmonious resonances, and the land of the Manes of the tombless dead—the land of nowhere.

ACKNOWLEDGMENTS

At the end of these peregrinations to mythical lands, I would like to profoundly thank my editor, Valérie Dumeige, for offering me to go on this beautiful journey in time and space, and for having been so invested in this nice project. I would also like to thank Karine Do Vale for her precise and efficient collaboration, and Karin Doering-Froger for her excellent creative work. All my thanks finally go to Stéfanie for being alongside me every day, for her smile, and for her constant encouragement. Thanks to all four; without you, this book simply would not exist.